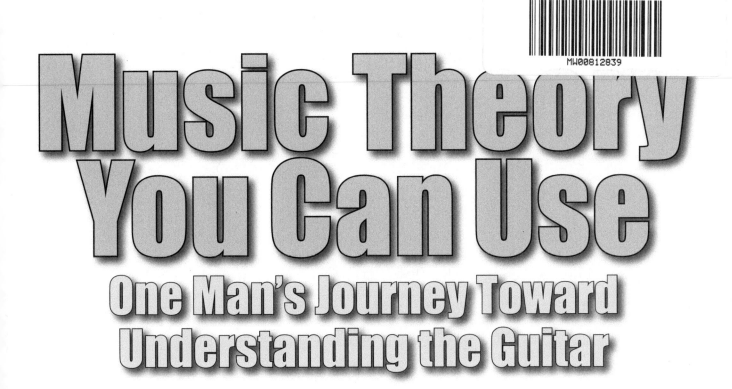

Music Theory You Can Use

One Man's Journey Toward Understanding the Guitar

Music Theory You Can Use

One Man's Journey Toward Understanding the Guitar

Steve Maase
Edited by Lily Maase

GUITAR DAD

Guitar Dad, LLC
Albuquerque, New Mexico 87102
www.TheoryForGuitar.com

For more information, please contact:
Mascot Books
560 Herndon Parkway #120
Herndon, VA 20170
info@mascotbooks.com

Library of Congress Control Number: 2017913322

PRINT: 978-1-68401-629-7

Printed in the United States of America

Cover artwork by Marcelo Gallegos
Steve Maase portrait photographs by Marita Weil
All other photographs reprinted with permission from the Maase family archive
Book Design by Scott Friedlander and Lily Maase with additional help from Wesley Jones

DEDICATION

In sitting down to find a way to properly introduce this book I am finding that, for the most part, my words escape me. For those of you who watched me grow up under my father's instruction and care you may find this, shall we say, unusual. I have long been known as a woman of many words. So, I will speak a bit about my family, and why we have come to fall in love with the guitar.

I began playing the guitar in 1989, at the age of seven. At the time it seemed, in many ways, almost impossible *not* to learn to play. The guitar—and particularly the electric guitar—was everywhere! Guns N' Roses' *Appetite for Destruction* had just hit the airwaves. Stevie Ray Vaughan was still alive and on the road. Nirvana hadn't even happened. Les Pauls and Stratocasters were on the cover of every magazine, on the newly-minted MTV, on almost every song on every popular radio station, and (most importantly) on every flat surface and in every closet of our modest New Mexican house, where I was raised by the inimitable session guitarist and educator Steve Maase.

The guitar was, and remains to this day, the most exciting and magical thing I have ever seen. The first time I picked the instrument up, it became an essential part of who I am, and who I will be for the rest of my life. As young as I was, I had to have one, I had to learn to play, and I had to be GREAT.

My name is Lily Maase. I am a guitarist and educator who has made a lifelong commitment to the craft of not just playing the guitar, but teaching it. But beyond this, I am Steve Maase's daughter. And as a result I am coming humbly to you, my fellow guitarist and student of music, with the legacy of a truly brilliant human being.

I spoke to my father for the last time on the afternoon of September 30, 2016, when he called to let me know he was about to hand in the final details for this book: various photographs, album covers and newspaper clippings that comprised the personal details of Steve's early life and career as a guitarist. We chatted briefly about his health (finally stable, after a brief bout with cancer three years prior) and next steps for the book (over twenty years in the making, it was almost done!), and made plans to speak the following day. This was the last conversation we ever had.

My father had turned 70 just two weeks prior, and had gotten in the habit of telling just about anyone who would listen that he intended to have his hands on his instrument until the day he died. I am happy to report to the people that knew and admired him that this was in fact the case; we learned of his passing because he was expected to perform at a club in downtown Albuquerque the evening of October 1st and never arrived. He had gone quietly in his sleep early that morning, his life's work finally finished and ready to share with the world.

My father worked tirelessly at every aspect of his craft, and yet he maintained that he had never worked a day in his life. At the peak of his career, I shadowed him at his studio as he taught 85-90 weekly students in half-hour increments; worked as a session guitarist recording jingles for national ad agencies and guitar solos for regional pop and gospel groups; spent hours in his workshop repairing electric and acoustic versions of the instrument; and, after all that, spent most weekend evenings onstage with a variety of bands, each of which rounded out the night at a local club with a minimum of three 60-minute sets.

At a time when young women by and large did not play the guitar, my father took me under his wing without indicating in any way that my interests were unusual. As a result I developed a confidence in and awareness of myself as a musician long before I was exposed to some of the realities that faced and still face the women in my field. I owe my father a great debt of gratitude for this, and when I think of him it is impossible for me not to think of this amazing instrument, the miracles that it has worked in my life, and what the guitar meant to both of us as fans of its music and students of its craft.

Beyond being the tool that keeps a roof over my head, the guitar seems to me a symbol of independence, of self-discovery and self-expression, and of the fact that it truly is possible for each of us to live in the world we create. It has been a solace and source of inspiration to 'outsiders' of almost every generation, a voice of protest for those who need to be heard, an expression of unity for those seeking common ground, and a tool of education that has reached thousands of people whose ways of thought fall just a little bit beyond the norm.

Above all this, because of the way it is constructed and the varieties of music that it calls home, the guitar truly is for anyone who has the desire to pick it up and play. The guitar is an instrument that belongs to the people. Every last one of us. As a result it lives and breathes in folk music, in jazz, in pop, in the blues, and at the very heart of rock & roll.

My father is perhaps the most perfect representation of what the guitar means that I have ever known. Here is a man who never went to music school—a man who taught himself to play beautifully and then, looking at what he learned, figured out how to take this information and share it with others. He did this selflessly, joyfully, and arguably at the expense of his own critical success. Here, also, is a man who came up through the tradition of the instrument *as that tradition was created*, who had brushes with fame alongside Buddy Holly, who remembered the earliest Fender amplifiers and guitars, who took the time to look at the guitar as it ascended into the pantheons of popular culture and ask an essential question: How does all this really work, and why?

When he was behind his instrument, Steve was a force of nature. But the thing that strikes me most upon reflection is the fact that, in his daily life, he was a flawlessly gentle and giving human being. He was unique, perhaps, in his conviction that the information that led to his successes also belonged to everyone he met along the way.

This book is a representation of all these things. In it you will find the beginnings of a personal memoir, not just of Steve's life but of the humble beginnings of popular music in the 1950s and 1960s. You will find an explanation of music theory so simple and so complete that, once you have worked your way through the material in the order that Steve suggested, it will seem bizarre that you did not have a mastery of this information all along. You will also find, in pursuing this knowledge, that you are left with more questions than answers, and that Steve's story leaves off at a point where it is certain there are still many things ahead.

This is where I come into the picture, for this book was intended not to be the completion of a story but the beginning. Steve left behind copious notes for a second volume, and outlines for several more to follow. I fully intend to use these notes and the success of this first publication to complete Steve's unfinished sequels and help them see the light of day. As you come to know me, I trust you will see that my father has taught me well.

One of the last things Steve said to me was this: "I am interested in teaching students, but at this point in my life I am more interested in teaching teachers how to teach." If you are a student of the instrument, I am convinced beyond a doubt that this book and its successors will give you access to the tools you need to continue on your journey. If you are a teacher like myself, it is my hope that you will come to see my father's work as the foundation for a tried-and-true method that will assist you as you endeavor to guide your students toward success.

Sincerest thanks to all of you who knew the inimitable Steve Maase and have entrusted me with the task of honoring the legacy of a truly remarkable man. I look forward to continuing to share a life of music and learning with you all.

With love,
Lily Maase, Guitarist

TABLE OF CONTENTS

INTRODUCTION

My students have always been my teachers. Their desire to learn has made me the teacher and player that I am today.

My approach to teaching has not been to teach them what I like or what I am interested in, but to teach them what they are interested in. When I start teaching new students, I ask them two questions:

- What got you interested in playing the guitar?
- What would you like to be able to play? (Songs, styles, artists)

From there, my 'process' begins.

I begin by showing them the things they will need to know in order to get them where they want to go; the tools that will enable them to play the music that is relevant to their lives. This puts the student in the role of being my teacher. I ask my students to bring in recordings of songs that they want to learn. Much of this music may be new to me—songs that I may not have heard by groups that might not be familiar.

Being blessed with a good ear, I do my best to figure out the songs and teach them to my students. Most songs have something unique about them: chord progressions, melodies, 'hooks,' approaches to improvising, and so on.

Then my other 'gift' comes into play: I am blessed with an inquisitive mind. I look at those unique aspects of the song and try to figure out how and why they work, what the musical 'logic' is behind them. If I have been successful in helping my students develop a desire to know these things, then I will share my knowledge of music theory with them.

In this way, my students have been a continuing source of exposure to new music—music that I might not have sought out on my own—allowing me to continue learning along with them.

This book is written for those who have that desire to know how the mechanics of music work.

Thank you for sharing your curiosity with me,
Steve Maase, Guitarist

CHAPTER ONE - PREFACE

My first exposure to playing music was taking piano lessons at age 8. I was growing up in Albuquerque, New Mexico, and many of the city's roads were simply trails cutting through the dust. It was 1954 and music was beginning to change. Rock and roll was on the verge of happening in America.

My mother was my teacher, which meant that she was always listening when I practiced, which didn't give me much opportunity to experiment on the piano. The times when my parents were out and I had the house to myself were the most enjoyable because I could just mess around and find things on my own.

This exposure to written music acquainted me with the major scale and the basics of reading standard notation. I never became a good sight reader. I would work my way through a piece of music and commit it to memory. From then on I wasn't reading the music; I was playing it from memory.

I plodded along through the first 3 or 4 books of the *John Thompson Piano Method* and learned to play using the same approach— struggling through reading the pieces and then committing them to memory as quickly as possible.

Steve's childhood home on Parsifal Street in Albuquerque, New Mexico, circa 1954.

I wasn't happy playing the piano, except for the few bits of 'free time' I had, when I would experiment with playing by ear. I would much rather have been outside playing with my friends than sitting on the piano bench playing songs that, for the most part, didn't interest me at all.

The exception to this was when my mother bought me a book of Count Basie's 'Boogie Woogie' piano pieces. The songs were more difficult than what I was used to, but parts of them caught my 'ear. I would experiment with similar things from my imagination, playing by ear instead of reading exactly what was on the page.

Around this time, at age 11, I was allowed to stop piano lessons. This was probably because my mother had taken me as far as she could with her teaching abilities and I didn't show enough desire to progress to warrant paying for a 'real' piano teacher.

About a year later, the summer before I started 8th grade, I got the idea that I wanted to play the guitar—partly because it was 'cool' and partly because my parents weren't wild about the idea.

My parents told me they would get me a guitar for my 13th birthday if I would agree to take lessons. I agreed, and they bought me a guitar. It was a small-sized acoustic guitar that cost about $25 and was painted

In Steve's own words, 'that geeky little kid at the piano,' toiling away.

gold with palm trees on it. Not what I had hoped for, but at least it was a guitar! They found a teacher: a 50-ish man, Mr. Becker, who came to the house on Wednesday evenings and began teaching me to read music for the guitar. We played songs like "Twinkle Twinkle Little Star" and other simple and familiar melodies from my childhood.

Needless to say, this didn't thrill me. I wanted to play the songs I heard on the radio—rock and roll!

After the first couple of months, Mr. Becker stopped coming. I was either a poor student or my parents, unhappy with my progress, had decided that the lessons were not a good investment. I did, however, still have my little Caribbean guitar. This left me on my own, without much guidance, but with a worthy instrument and a strong desire to learn to play.

By this time I had purchased, through mail order, a tiny transistor radio. The newest technology at that time, I could plug in the radio's earphone and listen to the rock and roll stations to my heart's content. All of these stations were AM stations. There were a couple of local radio stations that played rock and roll, but my favorite station was KOMA in Oklahoma City. Late at night, after the sun went down, I could pick up KOMA and I listened eagerly. They were a bit ahead of the curve in playing the latest songs, a blessing as the local stations in Albuquerque were a bit behind in their awareness of what was happening in the rest of the world. This radio was my constant companion, and as I absorbed the new sounds that came across the airwaves, I did my best to try to find them on my guitar.

My first successful attempt at learning a song on my own was a song called "Mule Skinner Blues". This was a Jimmy Rogers song, but the version I heard was by a guitar duo aptly called the Fendermen. One played a Fender Stratocaster, and the other a Telecaster. The song had a guitar solo that started at the 12th fret on the high E string and moved down the neck a fret or two at a time.

The Fendermen:
Jim Sundquist and Phil Humphrey.

It took a while, but I figured it out! This opened up a realm of possibilities for me: If I could figure this out on my own, I could probably figure out other songs on my own as well. This new-found ability was so exciting; I felt like I was finally going to be able to play what I wanted to play on my guitar!

I had no idea what I was really getting into but, as they say, 'ignorance is bliss'. It all seemed possible at the time, and although I was unaware of what the journey was to involve, I moved ahead with the confidence that I would succeed.

CHAPTER ONE - GETTING STARTED

One of the first things I learned when taking piano lessons was how to recognize notes on the piano keyboard. Every piano has white keys and black keys. The white keys represent the seven notes called 'naturals'; the black keys are called 'accidentals'.

The naturals are named using the first seven letters of the alphabet: A B C D E F G. The sequence then starts over in a higher octave (the 8th note is the same as the first, hence the term). The accidentals are described using the terms 'sharp' and 'flat'. Here's how this works:

- A 'sharp' (#) indicates that a note is to be played ½ step above the natural.
- A 'flat' (b) tells us that a note is played ½ step below the natural.
- A ½ step is the smallest musical subdivision. If you move from one note to the next closest note on an instrument, you will move an interval of ½ step.
- On the guitar, this means moving from one fret to the next, or from an open string to the first fret.

THE CHROMATIC SCALE

The guitar doesn't have the obvious advantage of having black and white keys; this means that, at first, the notes are a bit harder to see. To help with this, let's first look at them away from the instrument and then locate them on the fretboard once we understand how they are organized.

Each accidental can be named either as a sharp or flat. For example, the accidental between A and B can be looked at either as 'A#' (A raised ½ step) or 'Bb' (B lowered ½ step). Though they have different names, both of these notes sound the same. There is a special term for this; two notes that are spelled differently but sound the same are considered 'enharmonic'.

When all 12 notes (naturals and accidentals) are played in a consecutive order, the result is called the 'chromatic scale' (the word 'chromatic' means ½ step). The chromatic scale has 12 notes, which can be played over several octaves.

That's all there are—only 12 notes! How hard can it be to learn to use just 12 different notes? As guitarists, the answer is both 'very,' and 'not at all,' which is part of what makes the instrument such an adventure to learn.

Our first task will be to learn to see how these notes appear on the fingerboard of your guitar. As we have discussed, there are seven natural notes. There are also notes found in between the naturals. These notes are called accidentals.

If there were an accidental between each pair of notes, that should give us a total of **14** notes; however, there are only **12** notes in the chromatic scale.

*This is because there are two places in the chromatic scale where there are **no** accidentals between the naturals.* Those places are between the notes B and C, and between the notes E and F.

This can take some getting used to. The organization of whole steps and half steps looks like this:

A (A#/Bb) B C (C#/Bb) D (D#/Eb) E F (F#/Gb) G (G#/Ab) A

The chromatic scale can be started from any point without changing the nature or sound of the scale itself. For example, if you play your low E string open you have entered the chromatic scale from that note. Playing the first fret, ½ step above the E, gives you an F. The 2nd fret is F#, the 3rd fret is G, and so on.

Working through the chromatic scale along the low E string allows you to find and name any note on that string, so long as you remember which notes are separated by ½ step and which ones are separated by a whole step. When you reach the 12th fret, you will reach an E note one octave higher than the open string. All 12 notes are found on the 1st 12 frets; at the 12th fret the series repeats, and you can continue moving up the neck into the next octave.

The same thing can be done on each string, giving you access to all the notes on each string. **Diagrams 1**, **2**, **3**, **4** and **5** show you where the notes are found on the low E, A, D, G and B strings. The notes on the high E string are on the same frets as those on the low E string.

DIAGRAM 1:
Chromatic scale
on the E string

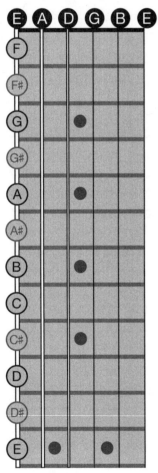

DIAGRAM 2:
Chromatic scale
on the A string

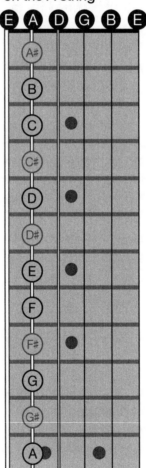

DIAGRAM 3:
Chromatic scale
on the D string

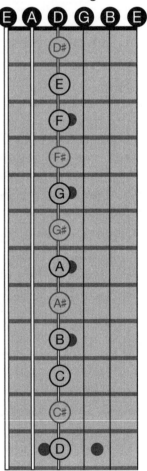

4

Being able to see where all the notes are may seem to be a formidable task, but as you work through this book, you will get to know them.

NOTE: *It is <u>not</u> necessary to memorize where all these notes are at this point. If guitarists had to name all the notes on the fingerboard as a prerequisite for learning the instrument, there wouldn't be many guitarists! Many beginning players, myself included, started on the instrument without having this knowledge.*

DIAGRAM 4:
Chromatic scale
on the G string

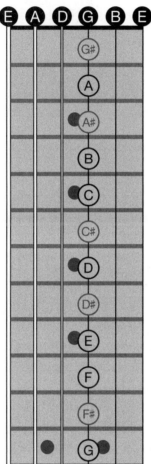

DIAGRAM 5:
Chromatic scale
on the B string

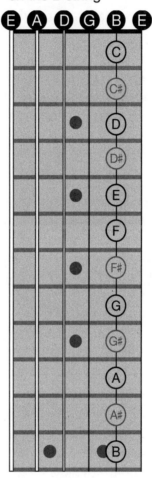

DIATONIC SCALES

While it is useful for acquainting us with the 12 notes available on the instrument, it is hard to hear melodies using the chromatic scale alone. The notes need to be organized in ways that are easier to hear and to use. There are many scales that organize these notes into different groups. Most of these scales are diatonic scales. For our purposes, diatonic scales are scales made up of seven different notes.

The most basic and most important of these is the major scale. The major scale is a sort of 'home base' to most thinking musicians; it also serves as the 'standard of comparison,' or our basis for looking at the way notes relate to each other. Much of the terminology used in describing chords and scales comes from the major scale.

There are many other types of scales, but the major scale is the most basic and easy to understand:

- A major scale can be started from any note in the chromatic scale.
- All major scales are alike in that they are constructed following a formula of whole steps and ½ steps. The location of the whole steps and ½ steps is as follows:

$$1 \quad {\scriptstyle 1} \quad 2 \quad {\scriptstyle 1} \quad 3 \quad {\scriptstyle ½} \quad 4 \quad {\scriptstyle 1} \quad 5 \quad {\scriptstyle 1} \quad 6 \quad {\scriptstyle 1} \quad 7 \quad {\scriptstyle ½} \quad 8$$

The numbered degrees of the scale are called intervals. By following this formula starting with the root note (the 1st interval), it is possible to build a major scale. Each note of the chromatic scale can be used as the root note of a different major scale.

All major scales are alike in that they follow the same pattern of whole steps and ½ steps. For example, the A major scale can be found by starting from the A note and following the formula:

$$\begin{array}{ccccccccccccccc}
A & & B & & C\# & & D & & E & & F\# & & G\# & & A \\
1 & {\scriptstyle 1} & 2 & {\scriptstyle 1} & 3 & {\scriptstyle ½} & 4 & {\scriptstyle 1} & 5 & {\scriptstyle 1} & 6 & {\scriptstyle 1} & 7 & {\scriptstyle ½} & 8
\end{array}$$

You will notice that the eighth note (called an octave) is the same as the first. A more detailed description of the major scales and their construction can be found in the Workbook section that follows this chapter.

FINDING SCALES ON YOUR GUITAR

An 'A major' scale can be played on the guitar by finding any A note and following the formula of whole steps and half steps up the string. For example, if you start with your open A (5th) string and move up the string following the formula, the result will be the A major scale **(Diagram 6)**.

The same scale can also be found by starting from the A note found at the fifth fret on the low E string **(Diagram 7)** or from any other A note on the guitar.

As you can see, there are many places on the fingerboard to play any scale. As you move through the book, you will learn many positions, but it is going to be best to start with one scale shape at a time and get to know it well before going on to the next.

DIAGRAM 6:
A major scale on
the A string

DIAGRAM 7:
A major scale
on the E string

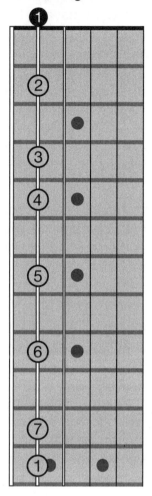

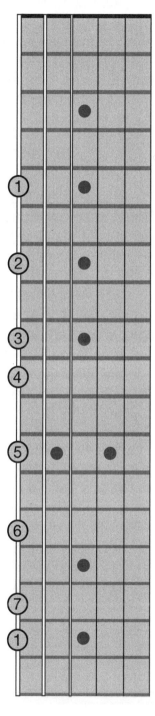

CROSS-TUNING YOUR INSTRUMENT

Before locating the major scale on the guitar, it is important to review how the instrument is tuned: Each string can be tuned to the 5th fret of the string below it. For example, playing the 5th fret on the low E string gives you the A note that is used to tune the open A string. The 5th fret on each string can be used to tune the next string until you need to tune the B string. The B note is found on the 4th fret of the G string.

This means that, in relationship to the other strings, the B string is tuned one ½ step lower. This will affect how we look at everything as it lays out on the fingerboard. (When tuning the high E string the 5th fret is used again.) This tuning approach is referred to as 'cross-tuning'. You can find diagrams showing this in detail in the workbook section following this chapter.

PLAYING THE MAJOR SCALE WITHIN A HAND POSITION

It is obvious that playing the major scale by moving up and down on the same string is not the most convenient approach. A more convenient way to play and visualize the major scale is to play it within a single hand position. A hand position is a four-finger, four-fret span, with the notes on each fret being played by one of four fingers.

Let's take what we know about the major scale and see how it takes shape within a hand position. For the moment, this is going to be much easier to see if we make an effort to stay away from the open strings. To make this easier, locate the A note at the 5th fret of the low E string. This is the root note of the A major scale.

Play this note with your 2nd finger. If you assign one finger to every fret, this will establish your hand position on frets 4 through 7, with each fret being played with fingers 1, 2, 3 and 4.

According to the formula, the 2nd interval is a whole step (two frets) above the root. If we stay in position, this note will be played with the 4th finger.

The 3rd note of the scale could be played one step above the 2nd on the same string **(Diagram 8)**, but in order to keep your hand position it should be played on the 4th fret of the A string. You will need your 1st finger for this one **(Diagram 9)**, which is why the position we established earlier is so crucial; using the four-fret span gives you the same note in a more convenient place.

This means that, within a given hand position, moving from the little finger on one string to the 1st finger on the next highest string is moving up a whole step in pitch.

By following both the formula and sticking to the four-fret span, you can now play a one-octave A major scale in position. The result can be seen in **Diagram 10**.

DIAGRAM 8:
Finding the 3 in
a hand position

DIAGRAM 9:
Beginning of the A
major scale position

DIAGRAM 10:
The A major scale,
1st octave in hand
position

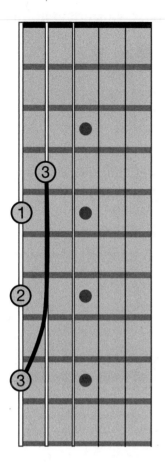

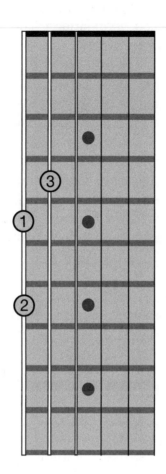

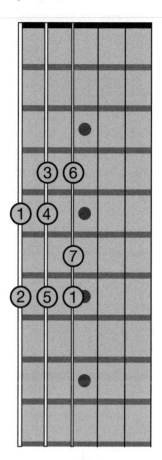

PLAYING THE MAJOR SCALE IN TWO OCTAVES

Keeping in mind that the 1st and 8th degrees of a scale are the same note, think of 8 as a 'new' 1 and use this as the starting point for the scale in the next octave. As you do this, remember that the B string is tuned ½ step lower in relation to the other strings. As you move from the 3rd string to the 2nd string the note on the 2nd string must be played ½ step higher to compensate for this difference. For example; to play a note a whole step higher than a note played on the 3rd string with the 4th finger, you would play it with the 2nd finger **(Diagram 11)**.

Now, starting from the octave A note, play the A scale in this higher octave. The result is the A major scale played over two octaves **(Diagram 12)**.

This gives us the **shape** of the major scale. *This shape or pattern is movable!*

9

If you want to play a C major scale, just find the note C on the low E string and, starting with your 2nd finger on that note, follow the shape. You will be playing the same intervals, but as they relate to the key of C **(Diagram 13)**. *Any* major scale can be played in this way. The root note may be different but the relationship of the notes to that root remains the same. The only variance to this occurs in scales involving open strings. The shape of a major scale starting from the open E string would be different **(Diagram 14)**.

The movability of these shapes gives us a big advantage as guitarists. It allows us to play any scale without having to think in terms of the note names. While the note names may be different in the different scales, the relationship of the notes to the root remains constant within the scale shape.

Learning to think of scales in terms of this relationship—namely, in terms of intervals—will let you see all major scales as being alike. Comparing an A major scale to a C major scale in terms of note names, you can see their differences. Looking at them in terms of intervals, you can see their similarities; they both follow the same formula of intervals. Using interval study to learn scales and chords is much easier than thinking only in terms of note names.

DIAGRAM 11:
The shape of a
whole step from the
G to the B string

DIAGRAM 12:
An A major scale
in two octaves

DIAGRAM 13:
The C major scale

DIAGRAM 14:
E major scale in
open position

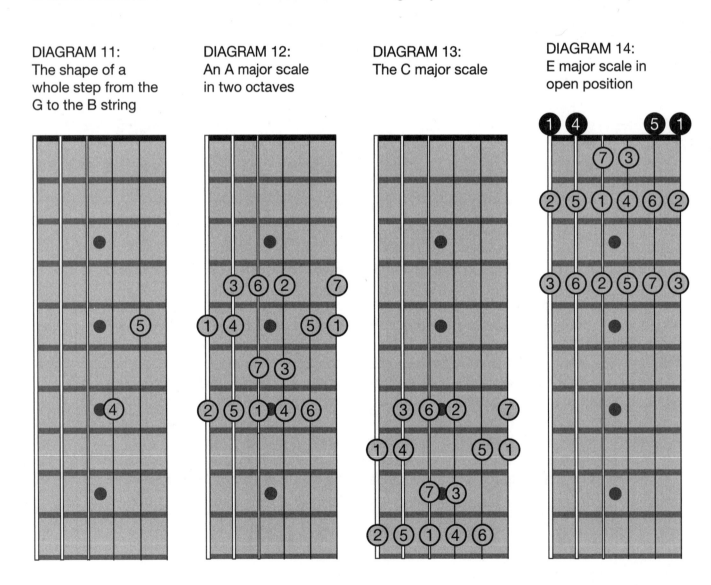

WHAT TO DO NEXT

Practice playing the shape of the major scale, taking the time to get to know the location of the intervals. Look for the ½ step points (between 3 and 4, and between 7 and 8) first. This will help you start to see the other intervals as you progress. Your goal is not just to memorize the shape of the scale, but to get to know the scale more intimately by seeing the formula and how the intervals take shape on your guitar.

Remember, the major scale is to serve as the standard of comparison, a window through which we can look at all other musical situations. If this foundation is not in place, all that is built upon it will be more difficult to understand. Study it, play it, experiment with it and, above all, listen to it. All major scales have a similar sound.

CHAPTER ONE - WORKBOOK

Most chapters of this book are followed by a Workbook section. They are divided into three parts:

- The **Information** section asks questions that highlight the important areas in the text. It may also give you written exercises to reinforce this information.
- The **Visualization** section contains exercises using neck diagrams. You will be asked to fill in scales or chords in the diagrams to help you visualize the concepts on the fingerboard.
- The **Application** section provides exercises designed to help you bring these concepts to your instrument. This section may have exercises with different levels of difficulty.

A WORD ABOUT THE IMPORTANCE OF THIS WORKBOOK

Anything of substance is built upon a solid foundation. The strength of that foundation determines how functional the rest of the project is. Just as the foundation supports what is built upon it, each consecutive step supports the steps that follow.

Some of you may have a tendency to skip over the basics in the first few chapters. At a first glance, what they contain may seem to be common knowledge and worth a quick glossing-over at best.

I would suggest that you take the time to read through the text in each chapter and do the exercises in each workbook section *in order*, especially if the concepts are relatively new. If you have already been exposed to this information, look at this as a necessary refresher before we forge ahead. There are many different ways of looking at these concepts as they relate to your guitar; the way this material is organized is crucial to your success.

Above all else, ***make sure your foundation is solid!***

INFORMATION

LEVEL ONE

In the chromatic scale, there are two places where natural notes are ½ step apart. What are those two places?

_____

_____

_____

_____

In the major scale formula there are two ½ steps. Between which intervals do these ½ steps occur?

_____

_____

_____

_____

What is the formula for the major scale?

_____

_____

_____

_____

LEVEL TWO

There are 15 different major scales: the C scale, which has no accidentals; seven scales that have one or more sharps; and seven scales that have one or more flats. Write out the scales as listed on the following page.

If this information is new to you, it may be difficult at first to determine which scales contain flats, and which scales contain sharps. What determines whether notes are named using the sharp name or the flat name?

The answer lies in what I have asked you to do. As you write out these scales, the letter names must be consecutive. *Never skip or repeat a letter.* If an E note is in the scale and the next note is a whole step higher, it would be called F#, not Gb. If an A note is in the scale and the next note is ½ step higher, it would be called Bb, not A#, and so on. To help you check your work, the correct number of accidentals is given to you for each key.

As the number of accidentals increases, you will encounter a situation where a C note needs to be called B# or an F note becomes E#. If a scale has an A# note with the next note being a whole step above it, that note appears to be a C. In order to follow the rule of consecutive lettering, however, it must be called B#. It looks like a C and sounds like a C but is called B#. This is one of the many uses of enharmonic spellings, which may appear to make some things more complicated than necessary. However, if we look closely at the intervals within the scale, we will see that using enharmonic spellings will often make it possible for us keep organized.

A similar thing occurs in flat keys. A Bb note followed by a note ½ step higher will require that the note that looks and sounds like a B will need to be called Cb. This is a bit confusing at first, but you will get used to it.

SHARP KEYS

	1	1	2	1	3	½	4	1	5	1	6	1	7	½	8
G (1#)	—		—		—		—		—		—		—		—
D (2#'s)	—		—		—		—		—		—		—		—
A (3#'s)	—		—		—		—		—		—		—		—
E (4#'s)	—		—		—		—		—		—		—		—
B (5#'s)	—		—		—		—		—		—		—		—
F# (6#'s)	—		—		—		—		—		—		—		—
C# (7#'s)	—		—		—		—		—		—		—		—

FLAT KEYS

	1	1	2	1	3	½	4	1	5	1	6	1	7	½	8
F (1b)	—		—		—		—		—		—		—		—
Bb (2b)	—		—		—		—		—		—		—		—
Eb (3b)	—		—		—		—		—		—		—		—
Ab (4b)	—		—		—		—		—		—		—		—
Db (5b)	—		—		—		—		—		—		—		—
Gb (6b)	—		—		—		—		—		—		—		—
Cb (7b)	—		—		—		—		—		—		—		—

VISUALIZATION

LEVEL ONE

The following diagrams show the cross-tuning process:

Cross-tuning: Using
the E string to tune
the A string

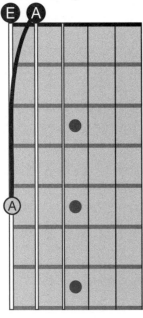

Cross-tuning: Using
the A string to tune
the D string

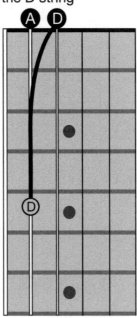

Cross-tuning: Using
the D string to tune
the G string

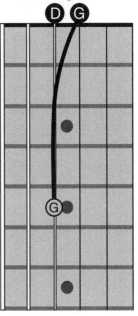

Cross-tuning: Using
the G string to tune
the B string

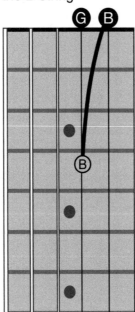

Cross-tuning: Using
the B string to tune
the E string

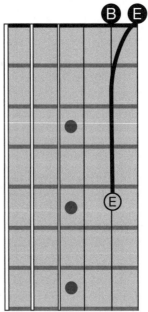

LEVEL TWO

<u>On the following three neck blanks:</u>

- Find a G note on the low E string.
- From that note, build a G major scale with all the notes on the E string.
- On the next neck blank, starting from that same note, find the G major scale within a four-finger hand position.
- On the next neck blank write out a C major scale within a four-finger, four-fret hand position.

G major scale
on the E string

G major scale with
root on the E string,
in hand position

C major scale with
root on the E string,
in hand position

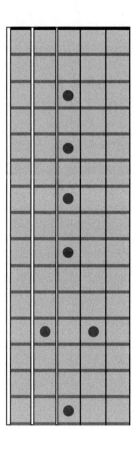
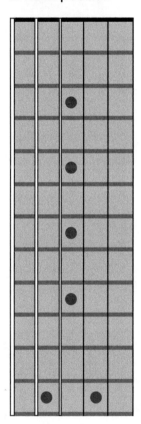
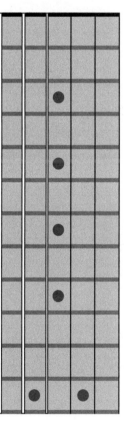

LEVEL THREE

<u>On the following two neck blanks:</u>

- Find a D note on the A string. From that note build a D major scale within a four-finger hand position.
- On the second neck blank, find an F note on the D string and build an F major scale within a four-finger hand position.

In both of these scales, the hand position will need to be moved up one fret when you move you the B string. This needs to be done to adjust for the tuning of the B string, just as we made the adjustment when we added the second octave to the major scale rooted on the E string.

D major scale
with root on the
A string, in hand
position

F major scale
with root on the
D string, in hand
position

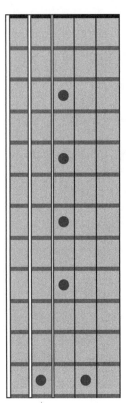
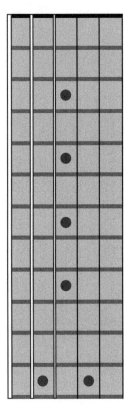

APPLICATION

LEVEL ONE

The major scale is the basis for other scales that we will be learning. The more familiar you are with the major scale shapes you have learned, the easier it will be to learn new scales in upcoming chapters.

As you work with the following exercises, keep in mind that it is important for you to be aware of the intervals you are playing. Don't just memorize the shape of the scale, discard the information that led us to the scale in the first place, and move on. This is a common pitfall for emerging guitarists!

Play the major scale ascending and descending several times. Begin slowly and be sure to keep an even tempo. As you work with these scales, always use alternate picking—down and up strokes. Never pick in the same direction twice in a row.

Play the scale again, but play each note twice, remembering to alternate your picking.

Now try playing each note three times.

Don't play the exercises too fast too soon. Never sacrifice clean, smooth execution for speed. Start at a comfortable tempo and gradually increase your speed. Practicing with a metronome will help you keep a steady tempo.

LEVEL TWO

Scales are necessary tools for writing and playing melodies, and are even more crucial for improvising. The notes in a given scale can be used in a variety of combinations to accomplish these ends. It will benefit you to practice scales grouping the notes in different ways so you don't get caught in the trap of only being able to play the notes consecutively.

Practice the major scale in groups of 3 notes. Starting with the root note, play a group of 3 *ascending* notes starting from each note in the scale.

1   2   3,

   2   3   4,

      3   4   5, and so on.

Then play 3-note groups *descending* through the scale.

8   7   6,

   7   6   5,

      6   5   4, and so on.

Once you have a handle on this one, try expanding the exercise by playing four consecutive notes instead of three.

CHAPTER TWO - PREFACE

My continued 'messing around' and my attempts to figure songs out by ear must have shown my mother that my fascination with the guitar might be more than a passing thing. If I wasn't going to take lessons, she thought that I should at the very least have some kind of access to what I wanted to learn. She bought me some guitar sheet music, which was way beyond my barely-existent reading abilities on the instrument. One of these was the song "Apache" by Jorgen Ingman, one of the few popular contemporary guitar instrumentals at that time. It was way over my head. I did learn the song (a bit later) but I learned it by ear, as I learned most things.

One of the other things she got for me was a basic chord book, which had diagrams of chords, mostly in open position (chords limited to the first three frets and/or using some open strings). This book was to prove invaluable.

Being blessed with a good ear, I was able to use this book to find chords that fit with some of the songs I heard on my transistor radio—songs by the Everly Brothers, the Kingston Trio, and so on.

And so the journey finally began in earnest. I knew that my ear had helped me to hear single notes; now chords were becoming available to me as well.

As I was learning to play my guitar I found that my musical interests were, to an extent, limited by my playing abilities. I was drawn to songs that I felt I could learn to play using my ability as an 'ear' player.

AM radio, which was all there was at the time (1959 to 1962), became my musical world. The AM stations were a source for the two genres that caught my interest—folk music and rock and roll. FM stereo radio was around in its early stages, but in Albuquerque the only(!) FM station aired classical music. This would change, but not for a while. My listening adventures were limited to the lower quality AM stations, broadcast in mono.

The first edition of Mel Bay's classic guitar chord dictionary, which is still in print today.

In my experience as a guitarist I have found that there are two basic types of players:
1. Those who are attracted to the instrument as a means of accompanying themselves or others while singing songs. These are primarily chordal players, with little interest in the more involved path of learning scales and becoming a 'lead' player.
2. Players who choose the path of learning to play lead guitar, often driven by their interest in the guitar as a solo instrument or as a vehicle for improvisation.

I loved the beat and guitar riffs by Bill Haley and the Comets and Chuck Berry and yearned to play them. But all those fast, fancy guitar riffs were way beyond my abilities at that time. All I had was my acoustic guitar, which lent itself to the less exciting (to me)—but more achievable—folk music. This was primarily played using open chords, largely the chords found in that basic chord book that my mom had given me.

I happily learned songs by the Kingston Trio, Peter Paul and Mary, and the Everly Brothers. I particularly liked the Everly Brothers, who kind of bridged the gap between country, folk and rock.

My pursuit of the guitar kindled a similar interest in a neighborhood friend. We found him a guitar in a pawn shop, and I taught him the basic chords and songs I already knew. We would spend time playing and singing folk music together. I found that I also had an ear for picking out vocal harmonies to these songs. This was to be my first step onto the path of becoming a guitar teacher.

I found pleasure and satisfaction in learning to play popular folk songs and could appreciate the stories told in the lyrics and the place that the music has had as an historic account of generations of 'common folk'—of their struggle and perseverance through difficult times, economically and sociologically. Folk music was important to the civil rights movement, the anti-war movement, and other socio-political causes that started to arise as I hit my teens.

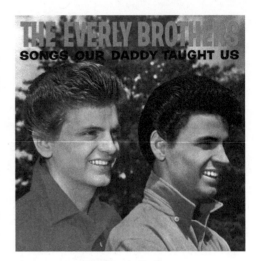

The Everly Brothers

While I enjoyed playing folk music, I was very strongly attracted to the more energetic and electric sounds of rock and roll. A lot of early rock music was very vocally-driven and the saxophone was the primary lead instrument. Doo-wop and vocal groups ruled the early 1950s and still didn't leave all that much room for the electric guitar.

But rock and roll began to shift its focus in the late 1950s primarily thanks to Chuck Berry, whose playing gave the electric guitar its most recognizable voice.

This music resonated in me in such a way that I knew this was for me. I had to learn how to play the guitar in this new way, so I could be a part of rock and roll.

However, until I could develop the skill to play chords and scales in different areas of the fingerboard my focus was on chords in open position—the chords used in folk music.

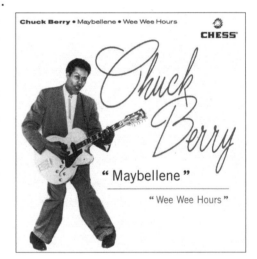

Chuck Berry

CHAPTER TWO - CHORDS: WHAT THEY ARE, AND HOW TO MAKE THEM

So, what *is* a chord?

Simply put, a <u>chord</u> is a group of notes that are played together—with a catch. If you have ever put random groups of notes together, you have probably encountered two extremes of sound. Some notes blend well together. This sound is <u>consonance</u>, or harmony. Some notes clash with each other. This is the sound of <u>dissonance</u>. Try putting random notes together on the guitar and see if you can find these two types of sound.

Even if you limit your experimentation to notes that we know are compatible—notes belonging to same the major scale, for instance—it is still possible for these notes to clash.

In our search for an understanding of chords, we need to start by finding consonant groups of notes. The search will be easier if we can define the terms 'consonance' and 'dissonance' a bit more clearly. A value judgment—saying that the consonant notes sound 'good' and the dissonant notes sound 'bad'—doesn't work. Dissonance is an important and unavoidable part of music and can be used constructively. The way to define and understand these terms is to look at what causes a given group of notes to sound a certain way.

Dissonance has a simple cause: It occurs when notes are played too close to each other. The closest together that two notes can be played is ½ step. Two notes played ½ step apart will sound dissonant. **Diagrams 15**, **16**, **17** and **18** are examples of notes that are dissonant when played together.

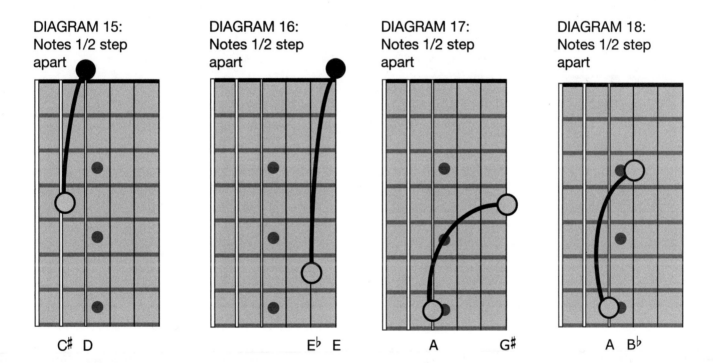

DIAGRAM 15:
Notes 1/2 step apart

C# D

DIAGRAM 16:
Notes 1/2 step apart

E♭ E

DIAGRAM 17:
Notes 1/2 step apart

A   G#

DIAGRAM 18:
Notes 1/2 step apart

A B♭

The ½ step is the most extreme example of dissonance. If you play notes that are a whole step apart instead, you will notice their dissonance decreases a little bit. If you continue to put more distance between the notes **(Diagram 19)** you will be moving away from dissonance into consonance.

In summary, we can define dissonance as the sound that occurs when notes are played too close to each other. Conversely, consonance is the sound that occurs when notes have some distance between them.

Dissonance and consonance are two inseparable parts of music. Music that is based on dissonance can sound harsh and grating, but music without it would sound bland, one-dimensional and emotionally shallow. The goal is to find a balance between the two, using a purposeful blend of both to create a myriad of tonal shapes and colors.

For example: If you play the notes in **Diagram 20**, they are audibly dissonant. But after adding some consonant notes—as seen in **Diagram 21**—the dissonance is still there, but it is not at all unpleasant. **Diagrams 22** and **23** give another example of dissonance being balanced by consonance. You will learn more about this as you build your first chord.

DIAGRAM 19:
Moving from dissonance toward consonance

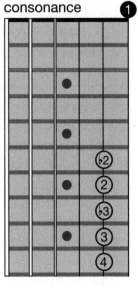

DIAGRAM 20:
Dissonant notes

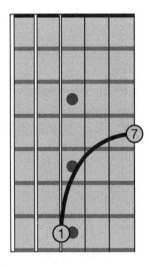

DIAGRAM 21:
Dissonant notes within a chord

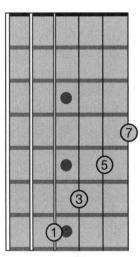

DIAGRAM 22:
Dissonant notes

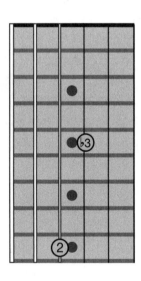

DIAGRAM 23:
Dissonant notes within a chord

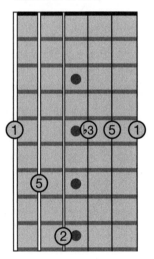

CONSTRUCTING YOUR FIRST CHORD

To make your first chord, let's start with the major scale and find notes within it that are as consonant with each other as possible. Remember that for our purposes, consonance = distance.

Starting with the root note, what note in the scale is as far away from 1 as possible? Remember, 1 and 8 are the same, so 7 is *not* the answer because 7 is ½ step away from 1(8). The answer must therefore be in the middle of the scale. Starting from 1, you can move all the way to 5 before we start moving closer to 1(8) again. The 5th (the distance from 1 to 5) is the most consonant interval that can be played.

This gives us the first two notes of our chord, 1 and 5:

<u>1</u> 1 2 1 3 ½ 4 1 <u>5</u> 1 6 1 7 ½ 8

The root and 5th are often played together as partial chords, sometimes referred to in rock music as <u>power chords</u>, or '5 chords'. Useful stuff, but the standard definition of a chord is three or more notes played together.

This means we haven't actually built a chord yet! We need to add that a third note to what we already have in order for the chord to be complete. In order to maintain the chord's consonance, this note needs to be as far away from 1 and 5 as possible. The only logical choice is the 3. All other scale notes are directly adjacent to either 1 or 5.

<u>1</u> 1 2 1 <u>3</u> ½ 4 1 <u>5</u> 1 6 1 7 ½ 8

This gives us our first chord, the <u>major triad</u>. It's called a triad because it contains three different notes. Because these notes come from the major scale, it is called a 'major triad'. To be even more specific, *the major triad is made by playing the 1st, 3rd, and 5th notes of the major scale.*

FINDING TRIADS ON THE GUITAR

Now that we understand how the chord is built, let's see how the major triad takes shape on the fingerboard of your guitar.

The chord shown in **Diagram 24** is an A chord. Why? First, its root note is the note A. With this in mind, in order for the chord to be a true 'A major' chord, every note in the chord has to be a 1, 3 or 5 of the A major scale. If you compare the chord to the A major scale shown in **Diagram 25**, you will see that this chord is indeed an A major triad.

You can see in **Diagram 26** that the triad intervals 1, 3, and 5 occur in the order 1 5 1 3 5 1, starting from the root note and moving across the fingerboard. Most of you are probably familiar with this chord. It is the shape of an open E chord moved up the neck.

The idea at this point is not to teach you how to play an A chord. That is the easy part. The value is in knowing *why* it is an A chord and where the components of the chord— the intervals—are located within the chord shape.

Another important thing that we have found is our first scale-chord relationship: a scale and the chord that can be found within it, or a chord and the scale that it came from—the scale that surrounds that chord.

If an E form A major chord occurs in a song that you are playing or writing and you want to write a melody line, bass line, or improvise over this chord, its scale contains the notes that are your creative tools. These are the creative tools that composers use when they write, and they can help you as you try to learn to play other people's songs. Understanding the chord-scale relationship can give you some insight into the creative process of other musicians you admire.

A great deal of what we will be doing throughout this book is centered around learning more chords, the scales that relate to them, and how to use them in practical, applied situations.

DIAGRAM 24:
A chord (E Form)

DIAGRAM 25:
A major scale
(E Form)

DIAGRAM 26:
A major chord
with intervals

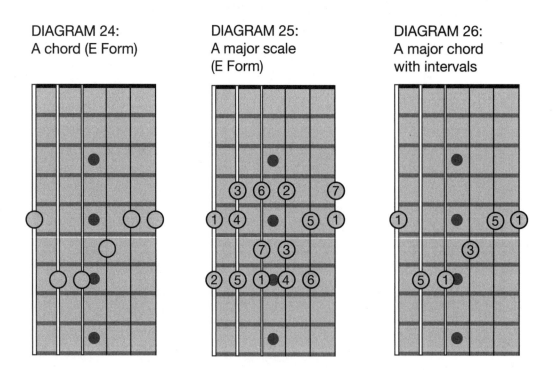

As we discussed earlier, the concept of movable shapes is crucial; it makes certain things accessible on the guitar in a way that is unique to the instrument. In our discussion of scales, we observed that the major scale shape can be moved up or down the fingerboard. While the root note changes, the relationship of the notes to that root remains constant. The same is true of chord shapes. This means that the shape of the chord in **Diagram 26** is movable! The root note is determined by the note played on the low E string, but the location of the triad intervals (1 3 5) remains the same: 1 5 1 3 5 1.

As you move the shape down the neck, you will find that in its lowest position it is an E chord. The intervals still occur as 1 5 1 3 5 1 **(Diagram 27)**.

If the guitar were tuned uniformly (all strings tuned to the 5th fret of the string below it) we could not only move the shape up the fingerboard, but also move it **across** the neck and still maintain the sequence of the intervals. It would be an A chord, with the open A string being the root of the chord.

The problem lies in the B string being tuned ½ step flat, as we discussed when looking at cross-tuning your guitar. We can move this shape across the fingerboard, however, if we compensate for this tuning discrepancy by raising the note on the B string one fret (½ step). The result is the A chord seen in **Diagram 28**. While the shape and fingering are different, the order of the intervals is the same—1 5 1 3 5 (1) with the higher '1' falling off the edge of the neck.

The shape of this open A chord can also be moved across the fingerboard by following the same idea: raise the note on the B string ½ step as you move the shape across. The result is the D chord seen in **Diagram 29**. The root note is the open D string, and the order of the intervals within the chord remains the same: 1 5 1 3 (5 1), with the higher 5 and 1 moving off the neck.

This gives us a group of three open major triads, a family of chords whose intervals occur in the same order: 1 5 1 3 5 1.

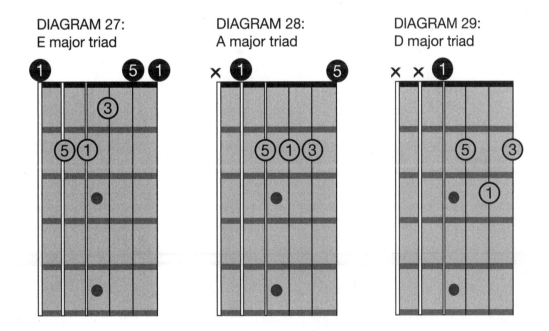

DIAGRAM 27:
E major triad

DIAGRAM 28:
A major triad

DIAGRAM 29:
D major triad

MINOR TRIADS

The major triad is used as the starting point for making other chords. This can be done by changing notes or adding notes to the chord.   The first example of this is the <u>minor triad</u>. In contrast with the major triad, the minor triad has a 'darker' or 'sadder' sound. A minor triad can be made by finding the 3rd in a major triad and lowering that note by ½ step.

| **Major triad =** | 1 | 3 | 5 |
| **Minor triad =** | 1 | b3 | 5 |

Let's take what we know and use it to change the E, A and D chords to minor chords. Find the 3 in the E chord and lower it ½ step to b3, as seen in **Diagrams 30** and **31**. Do the same thing with the A chord **(Diagrams 32** and **33)** and the D chord **(Diagrams 34** and **35)**.

The goal is to understand not just the mechanics of the chord shapes, but to understand the concepts behind them. If you can learn to do this, you are well on your way to expanding your chord vocabulary without having to memorize chord shapes. You will truly know the chords. Instead of relying on memorization, all you need to know is what the name of each chord means.

Chord names describe two things: the root of the chord, and then the formula, or the intervals that the chord contains. First, you need to learn what the chord formulas mean. Then, all you need to know is how to change the major triad to make each chord. Let's look at some of the most common formulas and get to work.

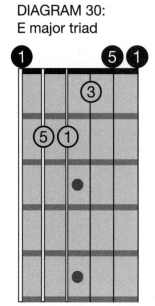

DIAGRAM 30:
E major triad

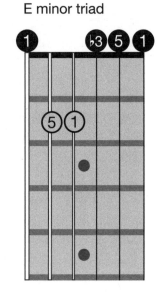

DIAGRAM 31:
E minor triad

DIAGRAM 32:
A major triad

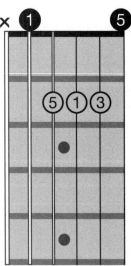

DIAGRAM 33:
A minor triad

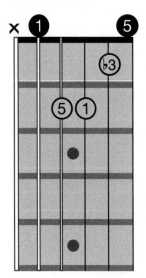

DIAGRAM 34:
D major triad

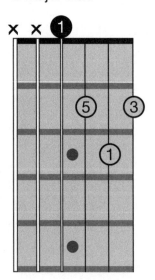

DIAGRAM 35:
D minor triad

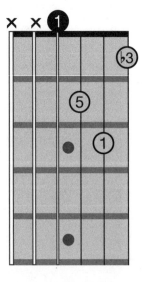

SEVENTH CHORDS

Major and minor triads serve as a foundation for building other chords. This is done by adding notes to the triads.

Keep in mind that chords are based on consonance. That consonance is maintained by building chords on every other note of the scale. Following this process means that the next note to be added is the 7th.

<u>**1**</u>　1　**2**　1　<u>**3**</u>　½　**4**　1　<u>**5**</u>　1　**6**　1　<u>**7**</u>　½　**8**

The resulting chords fall into the general category of <u>seventh chords</u>, which are chords that contain the root, 3rd, 5th and 7th degree of their parent scale.

There are three basic types of seventh chords:

- **The 7th chord:**   1   3   5   b7
- **The minor 7 chord:**   1   b3   5   b7
- **The major 7 chord:**   1   3   5   7

This is where the terminology can be confusing. There doesn't appear to be a direct connection between the name of a chord and the intervals it contains within it. Shouldn't a 7th chord have a 7? Why does it have a b7? If there is a logical connection between the chord and its name, shouldn't the 7th chord be 1 3 5 7? Let's look closer.

CHORD TERMINOLOGY

There is a logical connection between the intervals within a chord and its name, but there are a few things you need to understand about interpreting chord names before the logic becomes apparent. The difficulty lies in the fact that there are some parts of the chord that are implied, either because they don't need to be stated or because there is a problem in stating them.

The first thing that is implied is the major triad. If you are asked to play an A chord you might assume, correctly, that what is wanted is an A major triad. The phrase 'major triad', being the most fundamental chord, doesn't need to be stated. So we can say that, in a chord name, the letter itself (A, Eb, F#, etc) implies that you are to play a major triad based on that root note: A = 1 3 5

In the Amin chord the 'A' still means 1 3 5. But, the word 'minor' (min) gives us the additional direction that the 3rd is to be lowered by ½ step. In a chord's name, the term 'minor' always means b3.

Now let's look at the seventh chord, A7 (1 3 5 b7). If the 'A' tells us 1 3 5, then the '7' must tell us to add the b7 to the chord.

This doesn't seem to make sense: Shouldn't '7' mean simply '7'? If a chord has a b7 in it, shouldn't that b7 be stated in the name of the chord?

If the chord is called an Ab7 chord, the root note is not clear. Is the chord an A chord with a b7 added to it, or an Ab chord with a 7 added? This confuses the most important aspect of the chord's identity—its root.

At some time the judgment call was made that the easiest solution to this problem was to have the '7' imply the b7. This may take some getting used to, but '7' in a chord name always means b7. Hopefully, understanding the logic behind this will help you to keep this small but crucial detail straight.

The next chord, the <u>minor 7</u>, is now easy to interpret:

Amin7:

		1	3	5	
•	'A' tells us:	1	3	5	
•	'min' tells us:		b3		
•	'7' tells us:				b7
•	So 'Amin7' tells us:	1	b3	5	b7

The <u>major 7</u> chord is spelled 1 3 5 7. This chord seems like it should be called a 7th chord, since that is what it appears to be. But, the term '7' has already been used to describe the implied b7. This means the natural 7 is stated as what it is—the 7th note of the major scale. We will the chord 'major 7', or 'maj7' for short.

Amaj7:

		1	3	5	
•	'A' tells us:	1	3	5	
•	'maj7 tells us:				7
•	So Amaj7 tells us:	1	3	5	7

Let's review what we've learned:

		1	3	5	
•	The letter name means:	1	3	5	
•	'minor' means:		b3		
•	'7' means:				b7
•	'maj7' means:				7

Remember, abbreviations are often used for these terms.

- Minor can be 'min' or a lowercase 'm'. For instance, A minor might also be notated as 'Amin' or 'Am'
- Major can be 'maj'. For instance, A major 7 might also be notated as 'Amaj7'
- I have chosen to use 'min' for minor and 'maj' for major

There is no Workbook section for Chapter 2. Exercises involving the information in Chapters 2 and 3 will be found in the Workbook section after Chapter 3.

CHAPTER THREE - PREFACE

Is a good ear good enough?

A good ear is a *huge* part of what helped me along the path to a greater understanding of the fingerboard. My ear helped me to grow as a player, but was it enough by itself?

Granted, my ear is what really showed me that I could find things on my own, unaided by a teacher who wanted me to learn to play "Twinkle Twinkle Little Star". Method books weren't giving me what I wanted, but my ear alone wasn't giving me what I *needed*: an understanding of how the things I heard really worked. (I don't mean to say there is no value in learning to read standard notation; but for me, if notation been my only access to the guitar, I would have lost interest and my life would not have become what it has.)

Take, for instance, that first thing I learned on my own—the guitar solo to "Mule Skinner Blues". *If* my first teacher had known how to play it (which I doubt), it would have taken me months of lessons to be able to read well enough to learn that solo by notation, *if* I had been able to find a written transcription at all.

So...if my ear could teach me this much, why not just rely on it to learn everything else that I wanted to learn?

The ear needs to be 'educated' in order to hear more, and to hear more accurately. A large part of this education is facilitated by putting the correct labels on what you hear.

That first chord book my mother gave me showed me the way. As I learned to play these chords, I reached a new awareness. I could learn the chord shapes and try to get used to the way they sounded, but in order to use them to play the songs I wanted to learn—in order for my memory or my ear to recall them for use—I had to learn to label them correctly. To be able to hear the difference between major and minor chords, I had to name them and store them in my aural memory in order to recall them as needed.

Learning to hear the difference between a major triad and a minor triad served as a foundation for hearing other chords: the sound of a minor 7th, subtly different from a minor triad, or the sweet sound of a major 7 chord in contrast to the more dissonant sound of a 7th chord, the 'blues' chord.

What was it about the way these chords were made that gave them their distinctive sound?

I found that learning the theory behind the chord's construction—the intervals—helped me to hear them and then connect their names to their sound. By starting with the appropriate triad and then trying to hear what was added to it, I could figure out the chord and its name. This would also help me in connecting the right type of scale for finding melodies or for improvising, though I wasn't quite ready for that yet.

LEARNING THE LANGUAGE

As you play with other musicians, you will start to see the need to be able to communicate with them in terms that are not specific to the guitar. Learning a song written in tablature ('TAB' for short) is not going to help you communicate with a keyboardist or sax player.

Music theory is the language of music. It is a way that musicians talk to each other. Your ability to communicate with other musicians is enhanced by—or limited by—your knowledge of music theory.

CHAPTER THREE -
BUILDING CHORDS ON THE GUITAR

Let's take what we have learned and use it to make different kinds of chords on your guitar. Our goal is to start with the open E, A, and D chords and be able change them to minor, 7th, minor 7 and major 7 chords.

All we had to do to make a major chord into a minor chord was find the 3 and lower it ½ step. Making a 7th chord is a little more difficult.

A 7th chord contains the intervals 1, 3, 5 and b7. We know how to build the triad (1 3 5), so now we need to find the b7. There is no b7 in the major scale, but we can still locate it by looking between the 6 and the 7:

$$1 \quad {\scriptstyle 1} \quad 2 \quad {\scriptstyle 1} \quad 3 \quad {\scriptstyle ½} \quad 4 \quad {\scriptstyle 1} \quad 5 \quad {\scriptstyle 1} \quad 6 \quad {\scriptstyle ½} \quad (b7) \quad {\scriptstyle ½} \quad 7 \quad {\scriptstyle ½} \quad 8$$

As we discovered in the last chapter, the E chord is made up of 1, 3 and 5 in the order 1 5 1 3 5 1. You can use these intervals to find the b7. Looking at the scale above, you can see that the b7 is 1½ steps above the 5 and a whole step below the 1(8).

You can find the b7 by:

- **Raising 5 1½ steps**
- **Lowering 8(1) a whole step**

As you try the first of the two options on the E chord, you will see that there are two 5's to choose from. The 5 that is on the A string **(Diagram 36)** is not a workable option. Raising that 5 will add a b7 to the chord, but the fingering is not practical.

The other 5 is on the B string. It's much easier to add the b7 by raising this 5 1½ steps, as seen in **Diagram 37**. This results in an E7 chord.

The second option for making an E7 chord is to add the b7 by lowering 1(8) a whole step. While the E chord has three 1's in it, only the 1 that is on the D string can be lowered. Lowering this note a whole step (by lifting your third finger) makes the E7 chord shown in **Diagram 38**.

It is also possible to build an E7 chord using both options **(Diagram 39)**.

This brings up another advantage to understanding the intervals that it takes to make the chords: there are a variety of different ways that a chord can be played, or voiced.

As you will see, it is possible to voice any chord in many positions. Each of these voicings has a subtle character of its own. Learning to understand and voice chords in multiple positions allows you to select the chord that best suits your needs or the needs of a song.

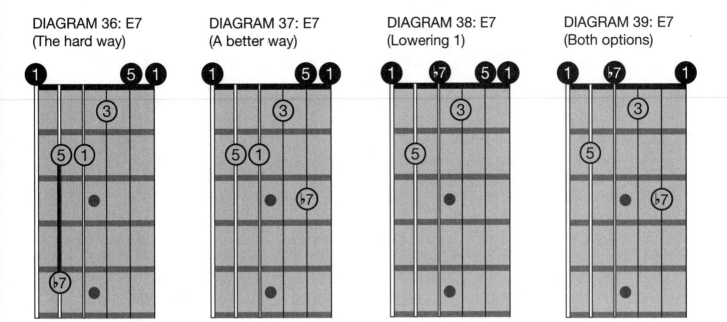

DIAGRAM 36: E7
(The hard way)

DIAGRAM 37: E7
(A better way)

DIAGRAM 38: E7
(Lowering 1)

DIAGRAM 39: E7
(Both options)

We can use this same approach to change the A chord to A7 by raising the 5 on the high E string 1½ steps **(Diagram 40)**, by lowering the 1 on the G string a whole step **(Diagram 41)**, or by using both approaches at once **(Diagram 42)**.

Moving on to the D chord, the 5 that we raised to b7 in the E and A chords has moved off the neck, so we only have the 2nd option available to us. The 1(8) that is on the B string can be lowered a whole step to b7, making the D7 chord in **Diagram 43**.

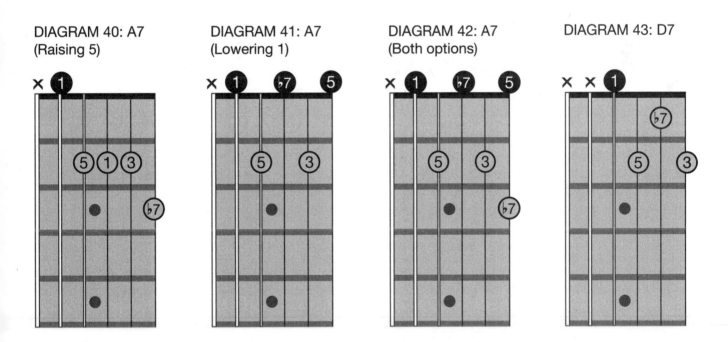

DIAGRAM 40: A7
(Raising 5)

DIAGRAM 41: A7
(Lowering 1)

DIAGRAM 42: A7
(Both options)

DIAGRAM 43: D7

MINOR 7 CHORDS

Minor 7 chords can be made by combining the steps you used to make the minor triads and the 7th chords. By looking at the name of the chord as a set of instructions, you can see how to make a minor 7 chord:

- 'minor' tells us to lower the 3 by ½ step
- '7' tells us to add the b7 to the chord, which can be done by raising 5, lowering 1, or both.

Diagrams 44-50 show the open E, A and D chords changed to minor 7 chords by following these two steps.

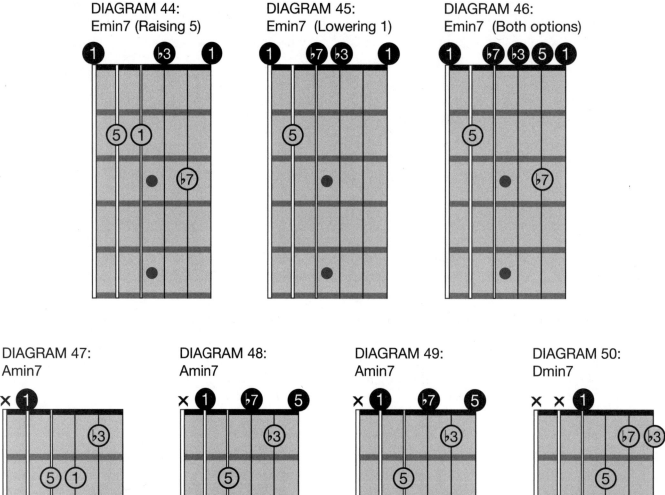

DIAGRAM 44:
Emin7 (Raising 5)

DIAGRAM 45:
Emin7 (Lowering 1)

DIAGRAM 46:
Emin7 (Both options)

DIAGRAM 47:
Amin7

DIAGRAM 48:
Amin7

DIAGRAM 49:
Amin7

DIAGRAM 50:
Dmin7

MAJOR 7 CHORDS

Major 7 chords are made, as the name tells us, by adding a 7 to the major triad. As you know from the major scale formula, the 7 is found ½ step below the 1(8). To make a major 7 chord, lower the 1(8) by ½ step as seen in **Diagrams 51-53**.

When making an Emaj7 chord, as in **Diagram 51**, the 1 on the high E string needs to be omitted. If you play a 1 above the 7 in a major 7 chord, the ½ step difference between the 1 and the 7 will cause dissonance, even if the 1 and 7 are in separate octaves.

DIAGRAM 51:
Emajor 7

DIAGRAM 52:
A major 7

DIAGRAM 53:
D major 7

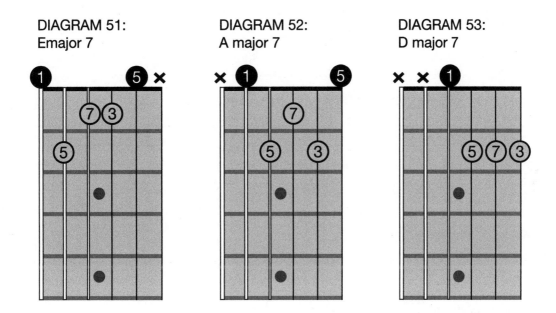

CHAPTERS TWO AND THREE - WORKBOOK

INFORMATION

LEVEL ONE

1. What is dissonance?

_____
_____
_____
_____

2. What is the most dissonant interval?

_____
_____
_____
_____

3. What is consonance?

_____
_____
_____
_____

4. What is the most consonant interval?

_____
_____
_____
_____

Write out the formulas for the following chords:

1. Major triad

_____

2. Minor triad

_____

3. 7th chord

_____

4. Minor 7 chord

_____

5. Major 7 chord

_____

VISUALIZATION

Even though you may be familiar with the open E, A, and D chords covered in these chapters, it is important that you do these exercises. Knowing how to play the chords is only part of the goal. It is important to know where the components of the chords—the intervals—are located. These chords are the basis for other chord types, many yet to be learned.

Having a good vocabulary is important, but there are so many different chords that learning them by memorization is a daunting task, even for those with excellent memories. The solution to this problem involves learning the process used to build chords. Writing out these chords will help you become more familiar with this process.

Use the following diagrams to build different kinds of open chords. Directions for placing the b7 are given. 'Lower 1' means 1 is to be lowered a whole step. 'Raise 5' tells you to raise the 5 1½ steps. 'Both places' tells you to add the b7 by using both approaches.

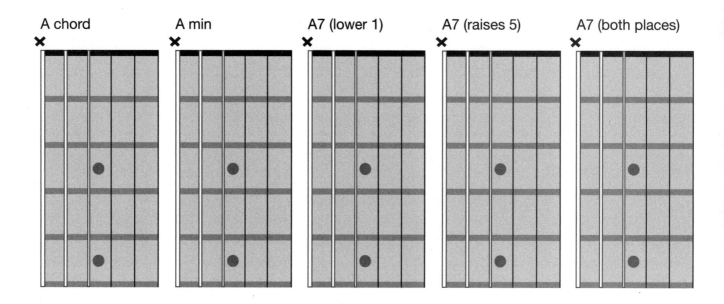

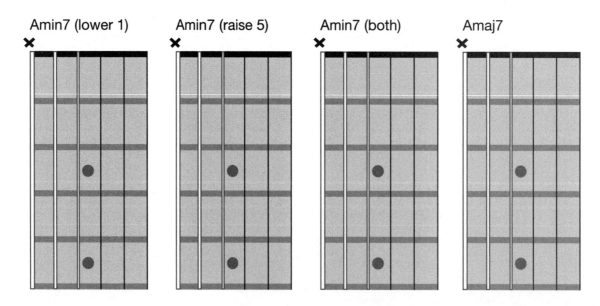

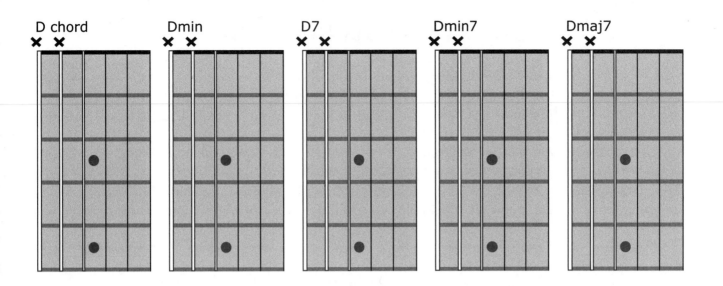

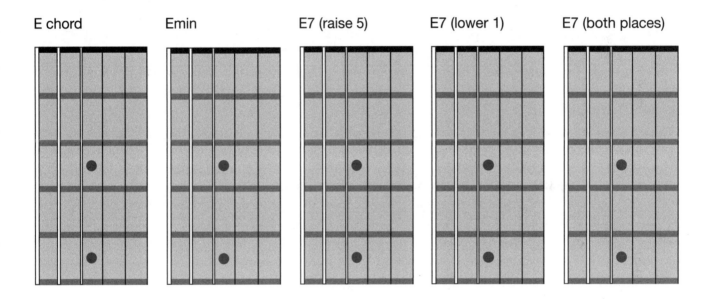

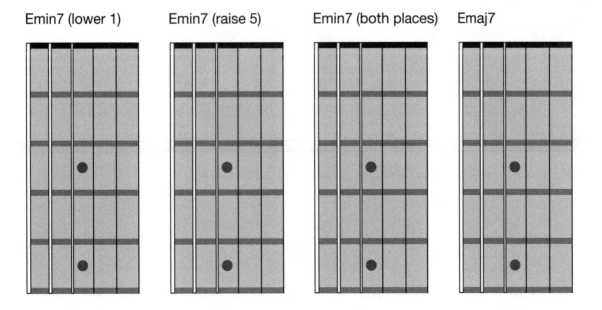

CHAPTER FOUR - PREFACE

Part of my 'education' as a young guitarist was to seek out other kids who played and get together with them to compare notes. I would share songs that I knew and trade information about the guitar; this made it possible for me to see what they knew that I didn't, and to share what I knew with them.

One of these kids was a classmate of mine named Bob. Bob had been taking lessons for a while; most of what he knew he had learned by sight-reading from basic method books. That didn't interest me, but he had also learned some chords. I soon discovered I could show him how to use these chords to play songs that were more fun to play than what he had been learning.

From this experience, I learned that my ear was a good teacher. Our chord knowledge was similar, but my ear had helped me use the chords to figure out how to play contemporary songs on my own, while he was using the *same chords* to play the simple (and boring) songs from his method book.

He could play one chord, however, that was totally new to me—an F chord. That was my first 'bar' chord. I had learned how to play a simpler F chord on the first 4 strings of my guitar from my basic chord book, but *this* F chord was different: it was made by barring across all 6 strings with my first finger and making the shape of the open E chord above the bar.

This was the most physically challenging thing that I had encountered on the instrument. Neither he nor I could execute this chord clearly and, at first, it didn't seem like it was going to be achievable at all.

Bob's guitar was a Harmony Archtone F-hole acoustic guitar—a more expensive guitar than mine. But, when we tried playing each other's guitars, I was surprised to find that my cheap little guitar—the equivalent of the Harmony Stella, their cheapest model—was the easier of the two to play! This was my first awareness that all guitars are *not created equal!*

Two different models manufactured by Harmony Guitars—the Archtone and the Stella. The Harmony guitar line was acquired by the Sears, Roebuck Company in 1916, who made them available in their department stores until the manufacturer went under in 1975.

CHAPTER FOUR - E, A, AND D CHORDS
AS MOVABLE SHAPES

So far we have learned how to change the open E, A and D chords to minor, 7th, minor 7 and major 7 chords. Let's take this information and expand on it so you can play *any* major, minor, 7th, minor 7 and major 7 chord in three different places on the fingerboard. This will be done by using these open chords as movable shapes.

You can move any open chord up the neck by barring across the fingerboard with your first finger. This raises the open strings. Then make the open chord shape above the bar with your remaining fingers, just like that F chord I learned from my friend Bob. As you move this shape up the neck, the intervals remain in the same location as in the open chords—our familiar 1 5 1 3 5 1. All that changes is the root note.

A bit about hand position: In order for the bar to work well, the first finger must be completely straight. This can only be accomplished by the thumb being in the right place: It should be behind the neck with the thumb joint straight, parallel to the frets, positioned only slightly up the neck from the bar finger.

Diagrams 54-56 show E form, A form and D form bar chords. The fingerings should be fairly obvious; however, in the A form chord, the three notes in the A chord shape can be played using fingers 2, 3 and 4 *or* by barring across those three strings with the third finger. This is the preferred fingering, but it may take some practice to be able to do this and have the high E string heard at the bar. The note on the high E string is the 5th of the chord. Since there is already another 5 played in the chord, you can still use this chord form while you are working on getting the high E string to sound.

DIAGRAM 54:
E form A chord

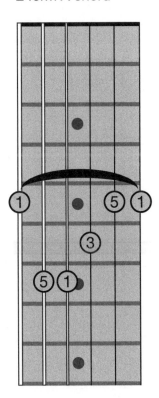

DIAGRAM 55:
A form D chord

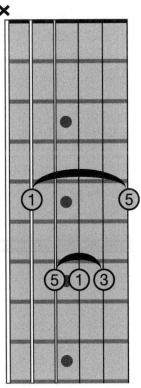

DIAGRAM 56:
D form G chord

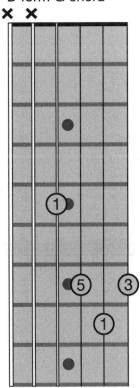

To practice finding chords in these three forms, follow these simple steps:

- Find the desired root note on the appropriate string. The root note of E form chords is found on the E string, the root of the A form chords is found on the A string, and the root of the D form chords is found on the D string. Using the location of notes at the position markers on each string **(Diagrams 57-59)** will help you find the root of any chord moving up the neck.
- Barring across that root note with your first finger, make the shape of the appropriate chord form above the bar.
- You can now change the chord as needed to make minor, 7th, minor 7, and major 7 chords the same way you changed the open chords.

DIAGRAM 57:
Notes at the dots
on the E string

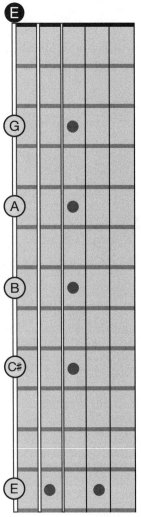

DIAGRAM 58:
Notes at the dots
on the A string

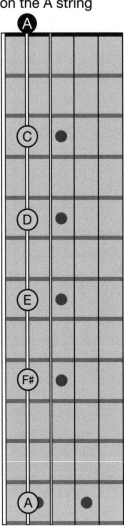

DIAGRAM 59:
Notes at the dots
on the D string

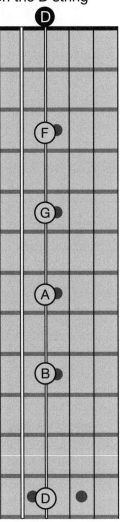

Diagrams 60-62 show an example of a Bmin7 chord found in three places on the fingerboard by using the E, A, and D form bar chords.

To practice this, choose random chords and locate them in three places on the fingerboard. Choose a root note, choose a chord type (major, minor, etc.), then find the chord on all three strings.

Examples and exercises expanding on this concept can be found in the Workbook.

DIAGRAM 60:
E form Bmin7

DIAGRAM 61:
A form Bmin7

DIAGRAM 62:
D form Bmin7

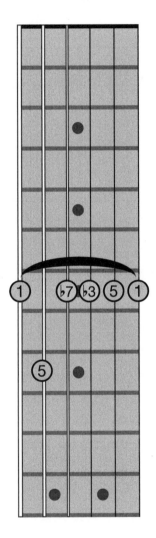

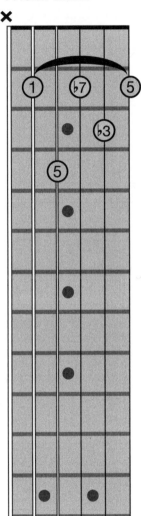

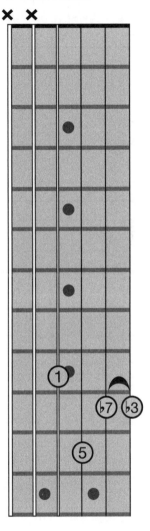

CHAPTER FOUR - WORKBOOK

INFORMATION

LEVEL ONE

In the terminology used in naming chords:

- What does 'minor' mean?

_____

_____

_____

_____

- What does '7' mean?

_____

_____

_____

_____

- What does 'minor 7' mean?

_____

_____

_____

_____

- What does 'major 7' mean?

_____

_____

_____

_____

- There are two approaches that can be used to add a 'b7' to a chord. What are they?

_____

_____

_____

_____

- How can you add a '7' to a chord?

_____

_____

_____

_____

VISUALIZATION

LEVEL ONE

Help with locating notes on the fingerboard:

As previously mentioned, notes are not as easy to find on the fingerboard of a guitar as they are on a piano keyboard.

While we have been spending our time learning chords and scales using note relationships (or intervals), it is still important to be able to see where the notes themselves are located. This is how we find the root notes of the chords and scales we will use.

In addition, because most musicians who play instruments other than the guitar learn by using note names, it is important to be able to speak their language. This allows you step into their world and communicate with them using familiar terms.

To help you work towards this goal, I am including some hints or 'reference points' that will help you develop the skill of finding notes on the guitar.

Reference Point One:

The first reference point is the open strings. By knowing the names of the open strings, you can find any note by moving up the string one fret at a time, using the chromatic scale, until you get to the desired note.

Reference Point Two:

While this first reference point is useful, it isn't always the easiest or most efficient way to find a single note. Sometimes a second reference point will be closer to the note you are looking for. This second reference point is the twelfth fret. On any string, the note at the twelfth fret is the same note as the open string, but it is one octave higher.

If you need to find a D note on the E string, it is easier to start at the twelfth fret and move down to D rather than starting from the open E and counting up the neck.

Reference Point Three:

The third reference point is the fifth fret. The fifth fret on any string, as we know from cross-tuning the guitar, is the same note as the next-highest open string. There is, of course, an exception when the G and B strings are involved; the note at the *fourth* fret of the G string is the same as the open B string.

Reference Point Four:

The fourth reference point is the seventh fret. The note at the seventh fret on the A string is an E, one octave above the E string. This remains true as you move across the fingerboard: the seventh fret of the D string is an A, and so on. Don't forget about the usual exception concerning the tuning of the G and B string. As a result, the G note on the B string is on the *eighth* fret instead of the seventh.

(See Diagrams on the following page)

Reference Point 1

E A D G B E

Reference Point 2

E A D G B E

Reference Point 3

A   B

B

A

Reference Point 4

E   G

E

G

LEVEL TWO

These exercises will help familiarize you with E, A and D chord forms as movable shapes. All examples are at the fifth fret. Remember that you can use these chord forms to play any chords you want by placing them at the proper fret.

On the following diagrams, write in the requested chords and number their intervals:

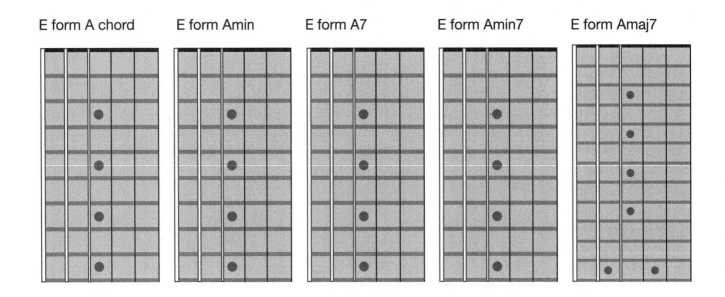

E form A chord   E form Amin   E form A7   E form Amin7   E form Amaj7

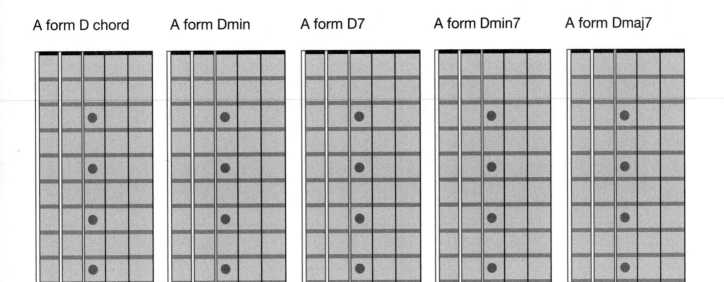

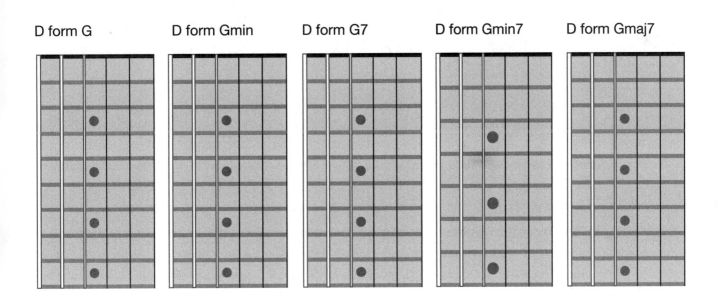

LEVEL THREE

The following exercise will help you learn to use the E, A, and D chord shapes to find a variety of chords in different places on the neck. The goal is to be able to find *any* major, minor, 7th, minor 7 and major 7 chords in three places.

On the neck blanks below, fill in the correct chord shape as indicated by the chord name above each blank.

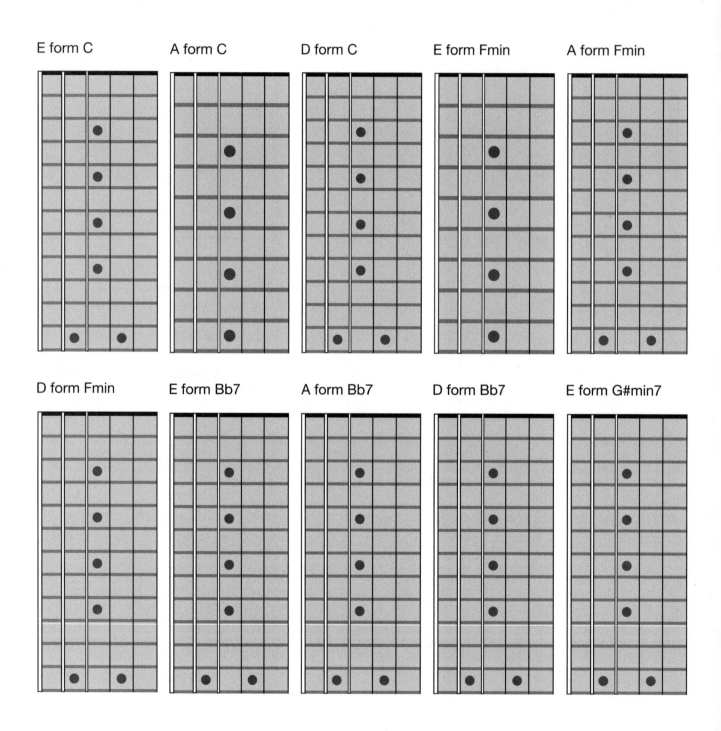

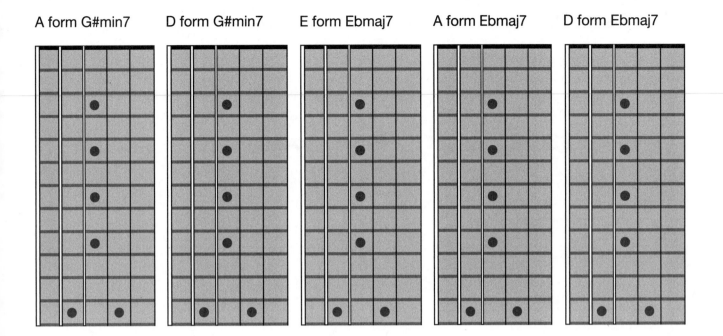

A form G#min7   D form G#min7   E form Ebmaj7   A form Ebmaj7   D form Ebmaj7

APPLICATION

LEVEL ONE

   There are two reasons for wanting to play chords in different places. One is the sound of the chord. Different chord forms give you access to higher or lower notes. The other reason is convenience, or <u>economy of movement</u>.

   For example: If a chord progression involves moving from a Gmin7 chord to a C chord, it can be done using E form chords for both. However, it is much more efficient to play the Gmin7 chord in E form and the C chord in A form. You could also play the Gmin7 in A form and the C in E form. See if you can locate both.

<u>Here are some progressions using all three chord forms we have learned:</u>

PROGRESSION:	**A**	**D**	**E**
Chord forms:	A (open)	D (open)	E (open)
Chord forms:	E	A	A

PROGRESSION:	**Dmin**	**Gmin**	**A7**
Chord forms:	E	A	A
Chord forms:	A	E	E

49

PROGRESSION:	Eb	Ab	Bb
Chord forms:	A	E	E
Chord forms:	D	D	E

PROGRESSION:	Cmaj7	Bmin	Amin7
Chord forms:	A	A	A
Chord forms	E	E	E
Chord forms:	E	E	D
Chord forms:	A	A	E

LEVEL TWO

Look for convenient ways to play the following progression. This time, you will have to figure out which chord forms to use on your own.

PROGRESSION:	Dmaj7	Bmin7	Emin7	A7

PROGRESSION:	Bmin7	Emin7	Cmaj7	Amin7

CHAPTER FIVE - PREFACE

THE BEGINNING OF MY OBSESSION
WITH THE INSTRUMENT ITSELF

My self-teaching continued. My playing must have started to sound like something because my parents 'borrowed' a better guitar from some friends whose son also played guitar and had outgrown this one. It was an 'Epiphone Jumbo Acoustic' guitar, the equivalent of a Gibson J-45. Epiphone guitars, at that time, were made by Gibson in their factory, which they sadly are not today. I wish I still had that guitar. It was a big step forward in terms of sound and playability, and it finally put those previously-unplayable bar chords within my grasp.

A Gibson J-45, the contemporary equivalent of Steve's first Epiphone Jumbo Acoustic.

Having a better-sounding guitar that was easier to play added fuel to my burning desire to master the instrument. Another thing that gave me further incentive was "The Adventures of Ozzie and Harriet," a TV sitcom centered around a real-life couple named Ozzie and Harriet Nelson. The Nelson family had a son named Ricky who was a real life guitar player and singer.

Ricky became a teen idol in real life, beyond the TV series. Every few episodes his playing and singing were woven into the plot, and Ricky Nelson and his band would close the show with a live performance.

I wasn't much interested in the plot of the show itself, but I would tune in to the last few minutes with hopes that I would catch what was the closest thing to a music video in those days.

More than Ricky strumming open chords and singing, it was his lead guitarist that caught my ear. This was none other than James Burton, the 'Master of the Telecaster' himself. This guy was playing all over the neck, not just in open position, and everything he played sounded amazing to me. How was he finding all those cool riffs? A mystery to be unraveled, but not for a while.

James Burton, the guitarist who arguably defined the sound of the Telecaster in American music, rose to popularity as the guitarist for Ricky Nelson on 'Ozzie and Harriet.'

James Burton was the real deal in those days. He went on to play with a number of different artists—Elvis Presley, Gram Parsons, and Emmylou Harris, to name a few.

His style of 'hybrid' picking—playing with a combination of a pick and fingers—was and still is an influence on many players, among them the late Roy Buchanan, the late Danny Gatton, Albert Lee, Brent Mason, John Jorgenson, Vince Gill and Steve Wariner. Several of these players can be seen together in the video of Eric Clapton's 2010 *Crossroads Guitar Festival*.

Seeing James Burton on TV gave me a strong desire to play electric guitar. After relentless begging and badgering, my parents took me to Montgomery Wards department store and spent $100 on an Airline 'Roy Smeck' Stratotone guitar. I was in heaven.

Steve's first electric guitar was a department store model, the 'Roy Smeck' Stratotone by Airline.

Montgomery Wards was a department store that was in competition with Sears and Roebuck. Each store had its own brands. The Sears musical instrument brand was Silvertone and the Wards brand was Airline. Both stores sold guitars under their brand names, but the guitars were usually made for them by other companies—primarily Harmony, DanElectro and Kay. These lesser-known guitars are sought after by collectors and players today, along with guitars made by Supro, National and a few other brands that fell out of favor over the years.

These 'entry-level' guitars were overshadowed in quality by the big players in the industry: Gibson, Fender, Gretsch, Guild, D'Angelico and Epiphone. These were all American-made instruments at the time. Their brand recognition is such that many of these names have resurfaced, but the instruments are *no longer* American made. Of these brands, only Fender and Gibson still make some of their better-quality instruments in this country.

Of the guitar amps that were made under these brand names, the Fender amps were the most desirable and were used by almost all of the pro players. Next in line were Ampeg amps, the closest to Fender in quality of sound and workmanship. The line still exists and is especially known for their bass amps, such as the SVT.

The history of these guitar and amp companies is fascinating and the development of these product lines is closely tied to the performers who used them. There are, of course, many guitars and amps that followed, but these are what were available at the time.

It may not have been a 'brand name' instrument, but I was thrilled to have my Roy Smeck guitar. I didn't, however, have an amp to play it through. My father had a reel-to-reel tape recorder and he let me use that to plug my guitar into. It wasn't very loud, but it worked fine for me for a while.

At this point in my search for more information, I was still dealing with shapes of chords and their names without understanding the theory behind them, the theory that we have been learning.

I also knew how to play (by ear) two major scales in open position—a C scale and a G scale—and could pick out some simple melodies as a result. Most of these were from simple songs by folk groups such as the Kingston Trio ("Tom Dooley") or the Everly Brothers ("Let it Be Me" or "All I Have to do is Dream"). These were well within the grasp of my still-growing ear.

I had no real sense of the connection between chords and scales, but I knew that there *must* be one somewhere. The melody to songs starting with a C chord could usually (but not always) be found within the C major scale. Similarly, in songs starting with a G chord, the G scale was the place to look for melodies. But, what about songs in other keys, or songs starting with 7th or minor chords?

I sensed that there had to be a connection between these chords and scales, but my ear and I were still pretty much in the dark. Things would have been easier for me back then if I had been able to see these relationships for what they were.

CHAPTER FIVE - THE SCALES OF THE THREE SEVENTH CHORDS

We have spent most of our time so far learning about different types of chords and how to find them in several places on the fingerboard. Before continuing to explore these chords, we need to bring our understanding of scales up to speed.

So far, we have only looked at the major scale and the chords that are found within it: the major triad and the major 7 chord. If you wanted to find or create a melody or improvise over these chords, the major scale is the tool that you would use.

What would happen if a 7th chord were played? Most of the notes in the major scale would sound fine, but the 7 in the major scale would clash with the b7 in the chord. This dissonance can be resolved by bringing the scale into agreement with the chord. The 7 in the major scale needs to be replaced with a b7. This new scale, a 7th scale, is the tool used to play over a 7th chord. Logical, isn't it? ***Chords and scales need to be in agreement with each other!*** Understanding this 'chord-scale relationship' is a crucial part of learning to think dynamically on the instrument.

Replacing the 7 with a b7 causes a shift in the location of the ½ step in our new scale.

Major Scale

1   1   2   1   3   ½   4   1   5   1   6   1   7   ½   8

(The ½ steps are between 3 & 4 and 7 & 8.)

Seventh Scale

1   1   2   1   3   ½   4   1   5   1   6   ½   b7   1   8

(The ½ steps are now between 3 & 4 and 6 & b7.)

Diagram 63 shows the familiar major scale shape with the root note on the Low E string.

Diagram 64 shows the scale with both the 7's in the scale replaced with b7's. You can see the ½ step is now between 6 and b7. You can also see that not all of the notes are played within the four-finger, four-fret hand position. When you move from the G string to the B string, the hand position is still there, but it is moved up one fret.

If a minor 7 chord is played, we must make another adjustment to bring the scale into agreement with the chord. In addition to replacing the 7 with a b7, the 3 also needs to be replaced with a b3.

Seventh Scale

1 ₁ 2 ₁ 3 ½ 4 ₁ 5 ₁ 6 ½ b7 ₁ 8

(The ½ steps are between 3 & 4 and 6 & b7.)

Minor Seventh Scale

1 ₁ 2 ½ b3 ₁ 4 ₁ 5 ₁ 6 ½ b7 ₁ 8

(The ½ steps are now between 2 & b3 and between 6 & b7.)

Diagram 65 shows the minor 7 scale. To play this scale, start with your first finger on the root note and then shift the four-finger, four-fret hand position back one fret as you move to the D string. You will need to move it up again as you move to the B string.

DIAGRAM 63:
E form Amaj scale

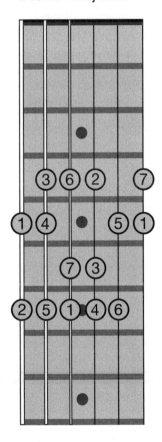

DIAGRAM 64:
E form A7 scale

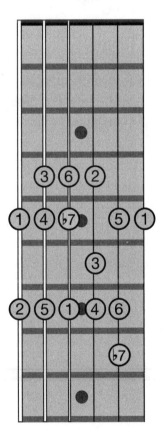

DIAGRAM 65:
E from Amin7 scale

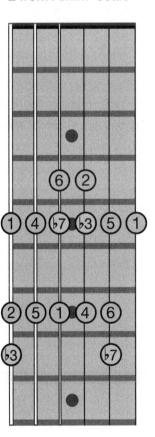

ARPEGGIOS

As you play these scales over their related chords, you will hear that some notes sound better to you than others: Some of the scale notes are dissonant with some of the notes in the chords. This occurs when a scale note is ½ step away from chord note.

For example: If a 7th chord is being played and you play the 6th note from the scale over it, you will hear the dissonance between the scale and the chord. The note wants to be <u>resolved</u> into one of the adjacent chord notes. This brings up the need for arpeggios when improvising or when writing a melody to fit a given chord.

In other words, **not all notes in the scale are equal**. The chord notes (1, 3 and 5) in the scale are obviously going to sound better against the chord, while the non-chord notes (2, 4 and 6) will tend to sound dissonant. An <u>arpeggio</u> is a chord played one note at a time. Playing a scale without the 2, 4, or 6 creates the arpeggio of that chord. When improvising, the chord notes are the primary notes and the 2, 4, and 6 can be looked at as passing notes, or notes that connect the chord notes.

- An A major triad arpeggio is shown in **Diagram 66**.

- An A minor triad arpeggio is shown in **Diagram 67**.

- An Amaj7 arpeggio is shown in **Diagram 68**.

- An A7 arpeggio is shown in **Diagram 69**.

- An Amin7 arpeggio is shown in **Diagram 70**.

Practice playing the scales of the three 7th chords and their arpeggios, making sure that you pay attention to the location of the intervals. The workbook section will give you some different ways to play the scales, which will help you get to know them better.

DIAGRAM 66:
E form A major
triad arpeggio

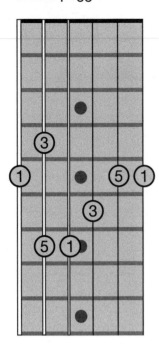

DIAGRAM 67:
A minor triad
arpeggio

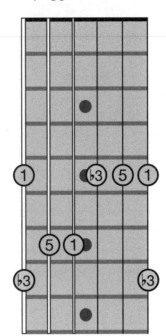

DIAGRAM 68:
Amaj7 arpeggio

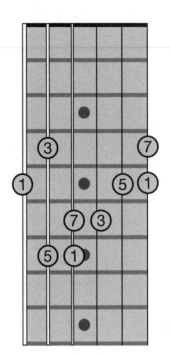

DIAGRAM 69:
A7 arpeggio

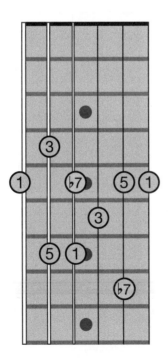

DIAGRAM 70:
Amin7 arpeggio

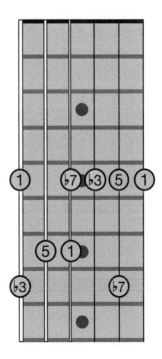

CHAPTER FIVE - WORKBOOK

INFORMATION

1. Where are the ½ steps in the major scale?

_____
_____
_____
_____

2. Where are the ½ steps in the 7th scale?

_____
_____
_____
_____

3. Where are the ½ steps in the minor 7 scale?

_____
_____
_____
_____

4. What is an arpeggio?

_____
_____
_____
_____

VISUALIZATION

LEVEL ONE

Write the following three scales on the neck blanks below. The root note should be on the low E string:

1. the C major scale
2. the G7 scale
3. Bbmin7 scale

E form C major

E form G7

E form Bbmin7

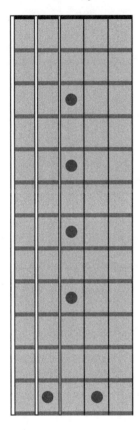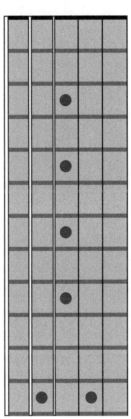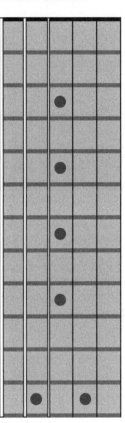

It is important that you do Level One, regardless of your experience on the instrument. Levels Two and Three are optional at this point. You can return to these exercises as you feel the desire to expand your picture of the fingerboard.

LEVEL TWO

Write the following three scales on the neck blanks below. The root note should be on the A string:

1. the C major scale
2. the G7 scale
3. Bbmin7 scale

A form C major

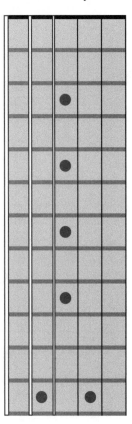

A form G7

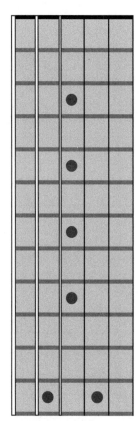

A form Bbmin7

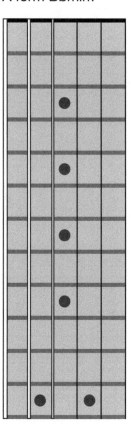

LEVEL THREE

Write the following three scales on the neck blanks below. The root note should be on the D string:

1. the C major scale
2. the G7 scale
3. Bbmin7 scale

D form C major

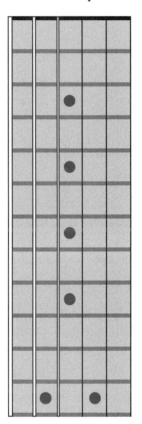

D form G7

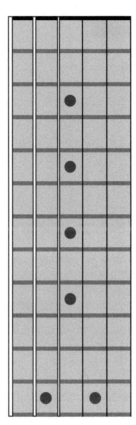

D form Bbmin7

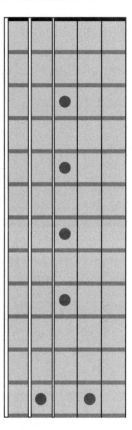

APPLICATION

LEVEL ONE

Practice the 7th and minor 7 scales in groups of three notes and four notes, ascending and descending as we did with the major scale in the workbook section of Chapter One.

LEVEL TWO

Here are some new ways to practice the scales you know:

First try playing the scales in 3-note groups:

Ascending: 3 2 1, 4 3 2, 5 4 3, 6 5 4, etc.

Descending: 6 7 8, 5 6 7, 4 5 6, 3 4 5, etc.

The scales can also be played in <u>thirds</u>. A third is found by skipping an interval as follows:

Ascending: 1 3, 2 4, 3 5, 4 6, etc.

Descending: 8 6, 7 5, 6 4, 5 3, etc.

LEVEL THREE

An important step toward successful improvisation is being able to look for melodic ideas within the scales you are playing. The following chord progressions—which should be repeated for practice purposes—can be used to work on developing this concept. Have a friend play the progression while you experiment with the scales. If you don't have someone to play the chords for you, use the recorder in your computer or another recording device.

Keep in mind that not all scale notes are going to sound resolved over every chord. Finding the notes that work will take some experimentation. Here's a hint: If you accidentally end a phrase on a dissonant note, try moving to the next scale note.

Use the A major scale to play over this progression:

Use the A7 scale to play over this progression:

Use the Amin7 scale to play over this progression:

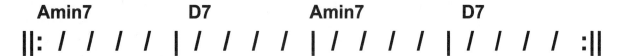

CHAPTER SIX - PREFACE

At the time (1958-1959), rock and roll was still primarily vocally-driven, accompanied by guitar, piano, bass, drums and often saxophone. While Chuck Berry had brought R&B guitar into the realm of rock and roll, his playing was still beyond my abilities.

One of the few exceptions to the current popular music format was a song called "Rumble" by Link Wray and his Wraymen. This was the first instrumental rock and roll song based around guitar that I had heard. It was recorded in 1958 and had the distinction of being the first instrumental to be banned by several radio stations out of fear that it would encourage gang fights ('rumbles') and other antisocial behavior.

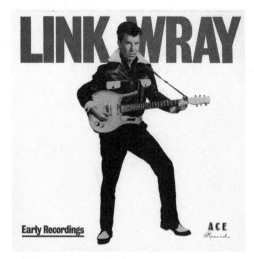

Link Wray's 'Rumble' was one of the first rock and roll songs to be banned by radio stations for ostensibly inciting 'antisocial' behavior among America's youth.

The song used open chords that I knew, and I was able to figure them out on my own. It also had a riff using notes from the first few frets and open strings. I figured these out with only a little difficulty. These notes, I would later learn, comprised an E minor pentatonic scale. This is probably the most important and usable scale a guitar player can learn, but for me at that time it was just a cool-sounding riff. I did, however, discover it could be moved up the neck, just like the other scales and chords I already knew.

Another appealing thing about this song was the tone of the guitar. It was *distorted!* I had never heard this sound come from a guitar before. Later on, I learned that Link Wray had achieved that sound by poking holes in his speaker with a pencil—an extreme way to find a tone that would become the defining sound of rock guitar!

By this time, I had outgrown the tape recorder I was using as a makeshift amp but didn't have the money to buy a proper one. Fate stepped in and solved the dilemma. My older brother Dan was working at a local TV station. One of the engineers at the station was building amps by copying the circuitry used by Fender. He had been doing this for some time and had a couple that he wanted to sell. The one that I liked was a copy of a Fender 'combo style' Bassman with a single 15" speaker. The tone was great. It was *loud* but it was heavy—the amp weighed over 50 pounds.

Steve's first amplifier was a 'bootleg' version of the famous Fender Bassman—a copy hand built by a local engineer.

In all, my little replica amp was a big step up from that tape recorder. It didn't have that great distorted sound that "Rumble" had, but I resisted the temptation to poke holes in the speaker (I actually thought about it). This amp lasted me for a while, until I could get a real Fender amplifier of my own.

CHAPTER SIX -
THE POWERFUL PENTATONIC SCALE

In the previous chapter, we discovered the scales of the three seventh chords. The notes within the scales were divided into two categories: the resolved notes (the chord tones—1, 3, 5 and 7) and the passing notes (2, 4, and 6). We make this distinction in an attempt to understand and ideally control dissonance—that sound that occurs when notes are played too close to each other in pitch, especially when they are ½ step apart.

If you look at the passing notes in the minor 7 scale and observe where the ½ steps are, you will see that the worst offenders for causing dissonance are the 2 and the 6. If you avoid playing these notes as you play the scale, you have played a minor 7 <u>pentatonic scale</u>. The scale, as the name implies, has only five different notes.

The Amin7 Diatonic scale

1   1   2   ½   3   1   4   1   5   1   6   ½   b7   1   8

The Amin7 Pentatonic scale

1   b3   4   5   b7   8

(Remember, 8 and 1 are the same notes.)

An Amin7 pentatonic scale with the root on the E string is shown in **Diagram 71**.

The same scale can be played in a shape that is stretched out more linearly on the fingerboard. This position starts from the b7, which is a whole step below the root. By playing the b7 and 1 on the E string (using fingers 1 and 3), moving over to the A string and playing b3 and 4, and then sliding the 3rd finger up two frets to 5, you will have the pentatonic scale shown in **Diagram 72**.

You can repeat this five-note shape in a second octave by moving your first finger over to the D string and playing the same shape starting from that note. This is shown in **Diagram 73**.

You can repeat this scale in a third octave, but be mindful of the tuning difference as you move to the B string. The first note of this octave has to be moved up a fret, but still played with the 1st finger. This is shown in **Diagram 74**.

Diagram 75 shows all three octaves of this 'linear' minor 7 pentatonic scale.

These 'E form' scales are found by starting from an A note on the low E string. The same scales can be found by starting from an A note on the A string. However, the shapes are difficult to see because they require you to use the open string. To make this easier, we will build the scale off the note D instead. These 'A form' scales can be seen in **Diagrams 76** and **77**.

The easiest way to play these linear scales is by using primarily the 1st and 3rd fingers.

DIAGRAM 71:
Amin 7 pentatonic scale

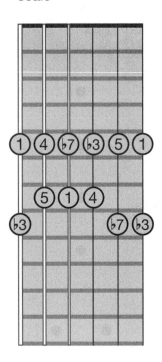

DIAGRAM 72:
Amin 7 pentatonic linear (lower oct)

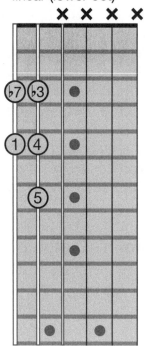

DIAGRAM 73:
Amin 7 pentatonic linear (middle oct)

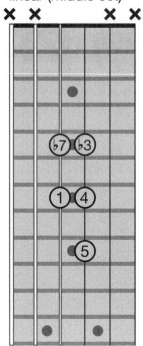

DIAGRAM 74:
Amin 7 pentatonic linear (upper oct)

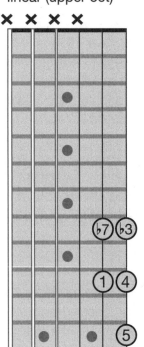

DIAGRAM 75:
Amin 7 pentatonic linear (3 oct)

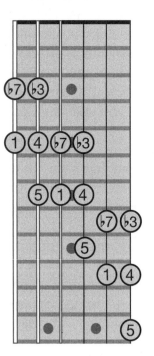

DIAGRAM 76:
Dmin 7 pentatonic scale (A form)

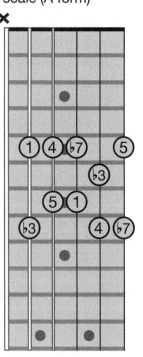

DIAGRAM 77:
Dmin 7 pentatonic linear (A form)

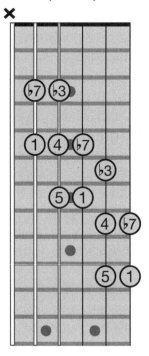

The pentatonic scale located within the hand position **(Diagram 71)** is easy to play since there are two notes on each string. Walking across the fingerboard using 1st and 3rd fingers or 1st and 4th fingers allows the hand to find an easy rhythm. Play the scale ascending and descending, then move around in the scale, moving up a few notes then down a few notes and try to find melodic ideas within the scale. You should also try playing the scale in groups of three notes and groups of four notes, similar to the exercises you have done with the diatonic scales. As always, try to keep track of the intervals you are playing.

The linear positions of these scales have some advantages. They not only give you access to some notes below and above the scale played in position, but they let you see the five notes of the pentatonic scale in groups that have the same shape and the same fingering. Practice moving through all three octaves as shown in **Diagram 75**. You can also play these scales in three-note groups. *Having the notes grouped like this means that, if you find a riff in one octave, you can play the same riff in the other octaves using the same fingering.*

Take these ideas and move them to the A form pentatonic scales. *Remember, these scale shapes are just as movable as the chords and other scales we have learned.*

Why do I say that the pentatonic scale is powerful? Its uses are vast. You can step from a pentatonic minor 7 scale into the diatonic minor 7 simply by adding the 2 and 6. The minor 7 pentatonic can be changed to a 7th pentatonic scale by replacing b3 with 3. Slurring the b3 to 3 gives us the beginning of a blues scale. Are you beginning to see the possibilities?

THE RELATIVE MINOR SCALE

There is a concept called the <u>relative minor</u> chord and scale. Every major chord (including major 7 and 7th chords) has a minor 7 chord that is located 1½ steps below its root. The pentatonic scale of this relative minor chord can be used as a <u>substitution scale</u> to improvise over that major chord.

Pretty cool! The minor 7 pentatonic scale can used to play over major chords if it is played in the proper relative minor position.

If this seems like a simple explanation for something far more complex, you're right. We will dig deeper into the relative minor concept a bit later when we learn about keys.

CHAPTER SIX - WORKBOOK

INFORMATION

The minor 7 pentatonic scale can be used to play over a minor 7 chord, or over chord progressions centered around that minor 7 chord. It can also be played as the relative minor scale to a major chord 1½ steps above it. With those things in mind, answer the following questions:

Amin is the relative minor of what chord?

_____

_____

_____

_____

Gmin is the relative minor of what chord?

_____

_____

_____

_____

What is the relative minor of Eb?

_____

_____

_____

_____

What is the relative minor of G?

_____

_____

_____

_____

VISUALIZATION

On the following neck blanks, write out the Gmin7 pentatonic scale. On the first neck blank, start with the root on the E string. Then, on the *same* neck blank, write out the scale with the root on the A string.

On the second neck blank, write out the linear shape of the Gmin7 pentatonic scale. Start on the b7, located a whole step below the root note on the E string. Then, on the *same* neck blank, write the scale out starting a whole step below the root note on the A string.

This will give you a picture of the Gmin7 pentatonic scale everywhere on the fingerboard.

Note: *I have encountered some people that suggest learning the pentatonic scale in 'five positions'. The approach that I have given you is easier to see, easier to play, and has a better practical application. It is where you will find the riffs that rock and blues players use.*

Gmin7 pentatonic
E form and A form
(in position)

Gmin7 pentatonic
E form and A form
(linear)

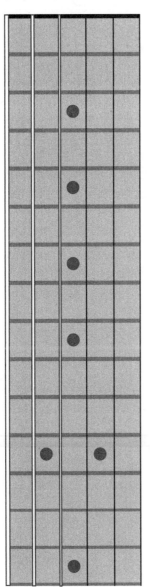
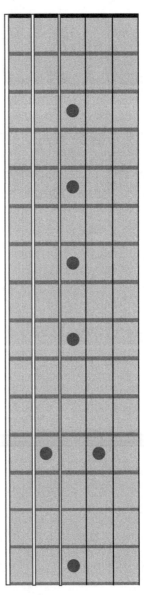

APPLICATION

Use the Amin7 pentatonic scale to play over these progressions:

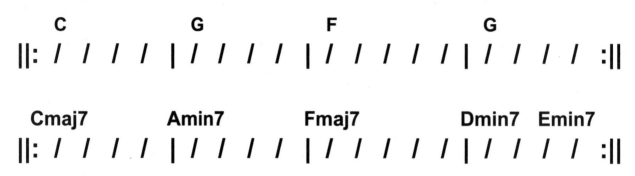

Amin7	D7	Amin7	D7
‖: / / / /	/ / / /	/ / / /	/ / / / :‖

Amin7	Emin7	Dmin7	F G
‖: / / / /	/ / / /	/ / / /	/ / / / :‖

Use the Amin7 pentatonic scale as the relative minor of C to play over these progressions:

C	G	F	G
‖: / / / /	/ / / /	/ / / /	/ / / / :‖

Cmaj7	Amin7	Fmaj7	Dmin7 Emin7
‖: / / / /	/ / / /	/ / / /	/ / / / :‖

Dissonance is still a possibility in these exercises. If you come to rest on a note that is dissonant, moving to the next adjacent note will usually resolve the conflict.

These progressions can be transposed to other keys and the same concepts can be used to improvise over them. Try these ideas to play over progressions to songs that you know.

CHAPTER SEVEN - PREFACE

The guitar had gotten ahold of me. I was beginning to spend all of my spare time practicing and trying to figure out songs by ear. The more I tried, the better I got. Every new thing I learned became part of my 'aural reference library,' stored knowledge which made each song easier to learn than the last.

Meanwhile, the guitar was finally beginning to play a larger role in rock and roll! Songs like "Angel Baby" by Rosie and the Originals and "Runaway" by Del Shannon used the guitar to establish their main themes. One of the most influential artists of the time was Buddy Holly, who wrote many of his songs around distinctive guitar riffs—both single notes ("Words of Love" and "That'll be the Day") and driving rhythm guitar ("Peggy Sue"). "La Bamba" by Richie Valens was another guitar-based song that is still played today. Santo and Johnny's instrumental "Sleep Walk" is another example of the guitar's first rise in pop music. Although the melody was played on steel guitar, I was able to figure out how to play it on my electric guitar using my developing ear.

When I was 14 or 15, I heard a song called "Walk Don't Run" by a group called the Ventures. The song was an instrumental, as were most of the group's songs throughout their long career.

The group had a basic line-up of two guitars, bass and drums. This lineup would be the basis for rock bands for years to come, and is my preferred configuration to this day. This was just what I needed: Rock music without vocals to get in the way of the guitars! It made things easier to hear, and I spent hours with my ears in front of a pair of stereo speakers.

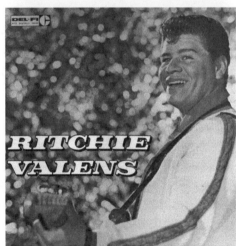

Buddy Holly and Richie Valens were at the forefront of the guitar's early days as the lead instrument in pop music and rock & roll.

Stereo was a relatively new phenomenon at that time. My older brother Dan, an electronics wizard, had put together a stereo record player from a kit. His ongoing quest for the latest in electronics was a big help to me. Many recordings were available in either mono or stereo at that time. Stereo albums were a bit more expensive ($3 for mono and $4 for stereo). For my purposes, having the guitars separated into two designated channels was worth the added expense. It made it that much easier to hear what was being played.

MOVING UP

As my playing got better, my parents became more supportive of my endeavors. My obsession with the Ventures drove my desire to have a Fender guitar, like my idols. They played Fender Jazzmaster and Stratocaster guitars and a Fender Precision Bass. These were beyond the means of a 15-year-old kid, but I figured that, if I could trade in my Roy Smeck electric and my Epiphone acoustic, I might be able to get a Fender Duosonic—a lower-priced, entry-level guitar.

I talked my plan over with my dad. He agreed to stop by the local Fender dealer, Riedling Music Co., on his way home from work and try to make the deal. The salesman, Clyde Hankins, told him they couldn't take two guitars in on trade for a lower-priced guitar. When my dad got home and told me the story, my heart sank. My dream was to go unrealized.

But my father went out to his car and came back inside carrying a rectangular Fender guitar case. I eagerly opened it up, overjoyed at the prospect of having the Duosonic after all. But inside the case, there was a beautiful sunburst Fender Jazzmaster! My dad had made a deal with Clyde to take both guitars in trade on the pricier ($402 at the time) Jazzmaster. There was, of course, a balance of $200 or so. Dad had paid the difference and expected me to pay him back in monthly payments, which I gladly did.

The Ventures, with their signature Fender Jazzmaster and Stratocaster guitars.

MY FIRST JAM SESSION

Shortly after I got the Jazzmaster, I received an invitation to a jam session with a piano player who lived three blocks from my house. I wasn't driving yet, so I walked to his house, carrying my 50-pound amp and my new guitar. There were four of us there: the piano player, a bass player, a drummer and myself. As it turned out, the bass player was a better guitarist than I was, so he ended up playing my new guitar and I played his bass.

This didn't make me very happy at the time, but wrapped up in this disappointment was something good—I learned that I had a strong enough ear to play bass guitar and added this to my pursuits. When I listened to music, I now not only tried to figure out the guitar parts, but could hear the bass parts as well.

The bass player stopped coming to the jam sessions, so I ended up playing guitar after all. We played for a few parties; then the piano player had to enlist in the Navy and that was the end of that, though he did play a few gigs with a group I joined later on.

Steve's high school photo, beloved Jazzmaster in hand.

TURNER SELECTS REFUEL PLACE ON RACE ROUTE

Famous Speed Flier Will Land at Colorado Springs on Los Angeles-Cleveland Flight

COLORADO SPRINGS, Colo., Aug. 26 (AP)—Colorado Springs will be a refueling point for Col. Roscoe Turner, famous speed flyer, in the Los Angeles-Cleveland air race scheduled for Monday.

Turner "boated" from Los Angeles to Colorado Springs in six hours Friday morning, inspected the mile square municipal airport and decided to make it his refueling point. He said the Pueblo airport, where he originally planned to stop, was too small for his fast ship.

After breakfast Turner departed for Los Angeles but left his representative, R. O. Pecoht, superintendent of an aircraft factory at Burbank, California, behind to complete arrangements for refueling. Pecoht said other entrants probably will decide to stop here instead of at Pueblo.

PURPORTED SUICIDE NOTE INJECTED INTO BERRIE HABEAS CORPUS FIGHT

MUSKOGEE, Okla., Aug. 26 (AP)—A purported suicide note was injected Friday into the habeas corpus fight of the Rev. S. A. Berrie, charged with the poison murder of his first wife, Mrs. Fannie Berrie.

The note, which defense attorneys said was found in a family Bible at the Berrie home, reads: "I am tired of life. It is not worth the effort. Goodbye forever, Fannie."

The attorney said specimens of Mrs. Berrie's handwriting would be presented in court in an effort to show that she wrote the note.

JOBLESS MEN DEMAND IMPORTED CREW OUSTED

SIDNEY, Neb., Aug. 26 (AP)—A large group of jobless men assembled at the court house here Friday and demanded that an imported crew of workmen, now employed on highway construction work east of here be discharged and replaced by Sidney men.

They said they had been promised work by Steel and Olinger, contractors, who they claim, brought their entire crew of workmen from a construction job at Ogallala.

The group soon dispersed.

Miss Marion Stull, overseer of the poor in Floyd county, Iowa, was kidnaped from her office in Charles City and beaten by a crowd of unemployed men who charged unfair distribution of wages paid by the county.

Kidnaped, Beaten

SYNDICATE TO CARRY OUT ITS SALES CONTRACT

SANTA FE, Aug. 26 (AP)—Warren R. Graham, state treasurer, was advised Friday that the syndicate holding the contract to sell $1,000,000 worth of New Mexico highway debentures would fulfill its contract and sell the remainder of the debentures.

Under an agreement the state treasurer will purchase $50,000 worth of debentures which remain unsold in the second block of $250,000 worth of debentures. The syndicate will make arrangements to sell the remaining two blocks, totaling $250,000 each, and will have until October 1 to sell the third block and November 1 to sell the fourth.

So far the syndicate has sold approximately $440,000 worth of debentures.

ROOSEVELT ENDORSED

those giving addresses were Orlando Ulibarri, candidate for sheriff, James R. O'Connor, A. A. Arresting at Olympia Hall Thursday, P. Sanchez and R. H. La day night endorsed Franklin D. Follette, for president. A dance was held after Roosevelt for president. Among the meeting. About 150 attended.

Riedling Music Company opened its doors in 1926 and was a mainstay of the Albuquerque music community for decades.

CHAPTER SEVEN - FILLING IN THE GAPS

SOME MORE CHORD FORMS

The E, A and D form chords and their accompanying scales allow you to find chords in several places on the fingerboard, but there are some gaps that these three forms leave. These gaps are filled by taking the open G, C and F chords and learning to play them as movable shapes.

Starting with the open G chord **(Diagram 78)**, let's find the scale that surrounds it. Starting from the note G on the low E string, follow the major scale formula, trying to stay within the first four frets. The resulting scale is shown in **Diagram 79**.

Comparing the chord shape to the scale, you can see that the triad intervals are found within the shape. However, they occur in a different order than in the E, A and D forms: 1 3 5 1 3 1 **(Diagram 80)**.

DIAGRAM 78:
Open G chord

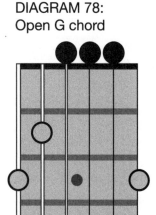

DIAGRAM 79:
Open G major scale

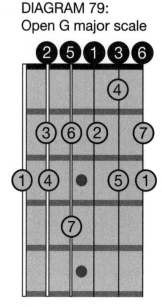

DIAGRAM 80:
Open G chord

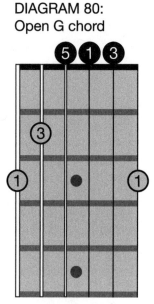

There is another way this chord is often played **(Diagram 81)**. This voicing moves the 3 that is on the B string up 1½ steps to a 5. While this fingering for the chord works well in open position, it doesn't move up the neck comfortably (not enough fingers), so we'll focus on the fingering in **Diagram 80**.

Let's move this chord across the fingerboard and, just as we did when moving the open E chord, raise the note on the B string to compensate for its tuning. The resulting chord is the open C chord shown in **Diagram 82**. The order of the intervals is the same as in the G chord: 1 3 5 1 3.

Moving this C chord across the fingerboard again and raising the note on the B string ½ step gives you an F chord, 1 3 5 1 **(Diagram 83)**. This F chord is often looked at not as a separate chord form, but as the upper four strings of an E form F chord. We will see a little later that there are advantages to both views.

The order in which the intervals occur in the open G and C chords is problematic: both chords contain two 3's. If we were to try and make these chords into minor chords, both 3's would have to be lowered ½ step to b3. One of the 3's in each chord is an open string and can't be lowered.

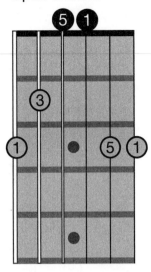

DIAGRAM 81:
Open G chord

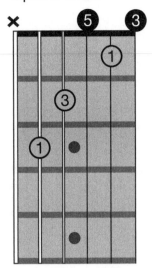

DIAGRAM 82:
Open C chord

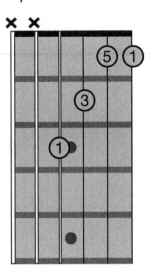

DIAGRAM 83:
Open F chord

As we move these chords up the neck as bar chords, the fingering problems continue to make the minor triads impractical.

Moving on to seventh chords, the G chord can be made into a major 7 chord by lowering the 1(8) on the high E string ½ step **(Diagram 84)** and a 7th chord by lowering the 7 ½ step **(Diagram 85)**. Minor 7 chords don't work because of the problem with having two 3's.

The open C chord can become a major 7 by lowering 1(8) by ½ step **(Diagram 86)**. Lowering this to b7 is not possible because the 7 is an open string. The b7 can be found by raising the 5 by 1½ steps to b7 **(Diagram 87)**. This eliminates the 5, but it is a compromise that will work for us. More about this later.

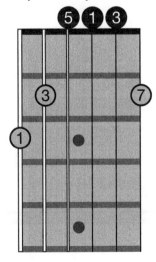

DIAGRAM 84:
Open Gmaj7 chord

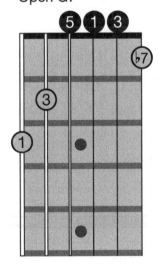

DIAGRAM 85:
Open G7

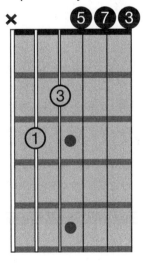

DIAGRAM 86:
Open Cmaj7

This 7th chord shape can be changed to a minor 7 chord if you don't play the high E string **(Diagram 88)**.

The F chord can be changed more easily to minor, major 7, 7th and minor 7 chords, as seen in **Diagrams 89-92**.

DIAGRAM 87:
Open C7 chord

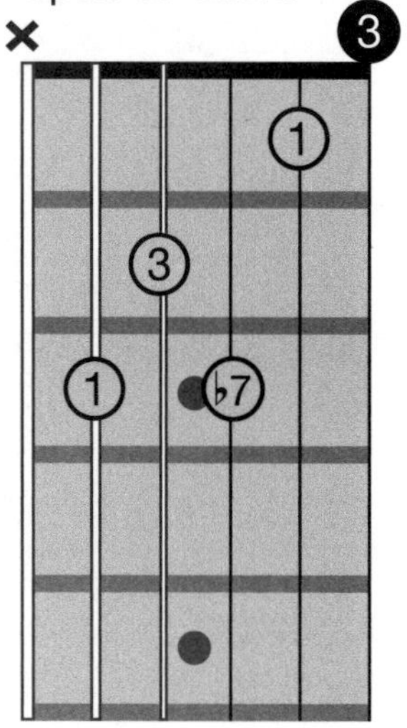

DIAGRAM 88:
Open Cmin7 chord

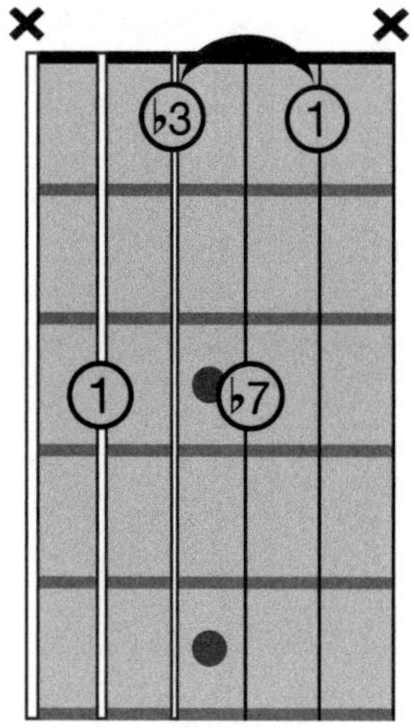

DIAGRAM 89:
Open Fmin chord

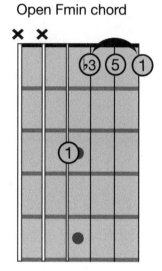

DIAGRAM 90:
Open Fmaj7 chord

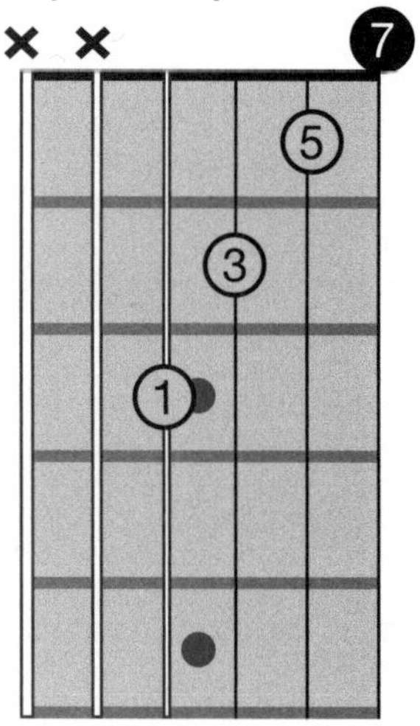

DIAGRAM 91:
Open F7 chord

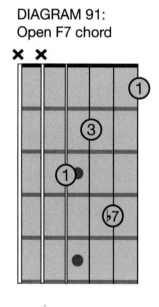

DIAGRAM 92:
Open Fmin7 chord

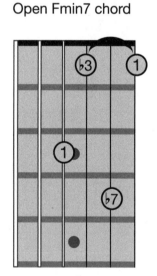

G, C, AND F CHORDS AS MOVABLE SHAPES

Just as the E, A and D chords can be moved up the neck to make other chords, the G, C and F chords can be moved as well. Let's start with the G chord: By playing the A note on the E string with your little finger and barring across the second fret with your first, you can make the G form A chord **(Diagram 93)**. The triad intervals occur as 1 3 5 1 3 1. This order occurs in the C form D chord **(Diagram 94)** and the F form G chord **(Diagram 95)**.

DIAGRAM 93:
G form A chord

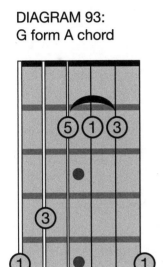

DIAGRAM 94:
C form D chord

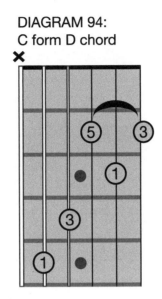

DIAGRAM 95:
F form G chord

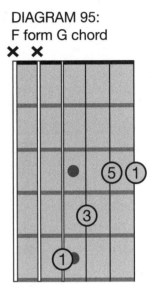

The G form A chord can be changed to major 7 and 7th chords just as the open chords were changed **(Diagrams 96** and **97)**. The fingerings are a bit awkward, but they will work.

DIAGRAM 96:
G form Amaj7

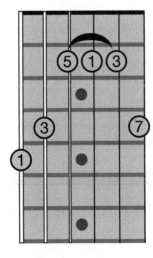

DIAGRAM 97:
G form A7

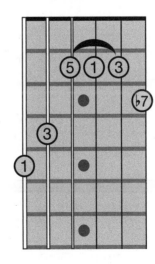

The same is true of the C form D chords. These chords can become major 7, 7th and minor 7 chords, as seen in **Diagrams 98-100**.

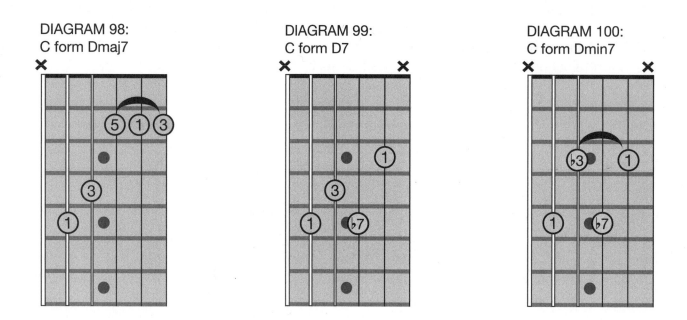

DIAGRAM 98:
C form Dmaj7

DIAGRAM 99:
C form D7

DIAGRAM 100:
C form Dmin7

The F form G chords can be changed to minor, major 7, 7th and minor 7 chords as shown in **Diagrams 101-104**.

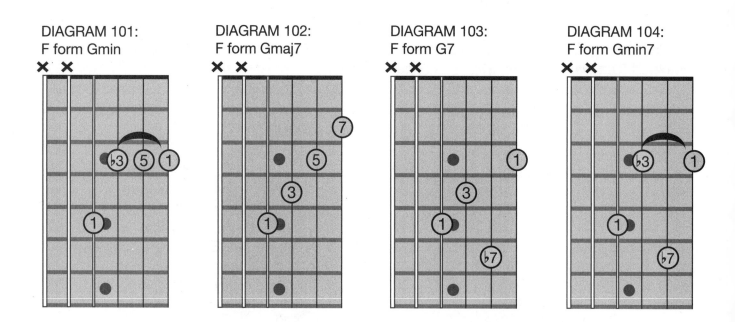

DIAGRAM 101:
F form Gmin

DIAGRAM 102:
F form Gmaj7

DIAGRAM 103:
F form G7

DIAGRAM 104:
F form Gmin7

When comparing the E, A, D chord group and the G, C, F chord group, you will notice a couple of distinct differences. The most obvious is the different order in which the triad intervals occur. In the E, A, D group they occur as 1 5 1 3 5 1. In the G, C, F group they occur as 1 3 5 1 3 1. As we have discussed, this makes changing the chords in the G, C, F group a bit more difficult.

You will also see that, while the notes in the E, A, D group are placed up the neck starting from the root, the notes in the G, C, F group are placed toward the nut. It may take a while to not look at the bar finger in the G, C, F group as determining the root.

This means that chords from both groups find their root notes on the E, A and D strings. Any note found on the low E string can be used as the root note for both the E form and G form chords, as seen in **Diagram 105**. Notes found on the A string can be used to play both the A form and C form chords **(Diagram 106)**. Both D and F form chords can be made from notes on the D string **(Diagram 107)**.

Combining the shapes in the proper sequence will allow you to find any chord you need anywhere on the fingerboard. Let's see how this works.

DIAGRAM 105:
A chord, G and
E forms

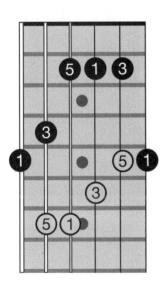

DIAGRAM 106:
D chord, C and
A forms

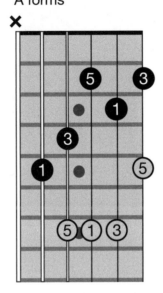

DIAGRAM 107:
G chord, F and
D forms

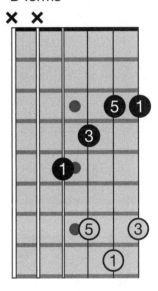

THE 'CAGED' SYSTEM

Let's start by finding a C chord everywhere on the neck. Starting with an open C chord, the sequence in which these chord forms occur up the neck is: C form, A form, G form, E form and D form **(Diagrams 108-112)**. As you can see, the forms in this order spell the word "CAGED". They will always occur in this sequence. The order can be started from any form, ascending or descending. I'm not sure where or when I first encountered the CAGED system, but it has been around for a while.

This approach not only gives us the ability to play any chord everywhere on the neck, it also allows us to play different chords in the same area of the neck. This keeps us from having to jump from one area of the neck to another unnecessarily.

Let's look, for instance, at the progression Emaj7, G#min7, C#min7, A, B. Find the root notes of each chord in the progression in the same area of the fingerboard, as seen in **Diagram 113**. Choose the chord forms from those notes, using the forms that will let you play the chords as close to each other as possible.

DIAGRAM 108:
Open C chord

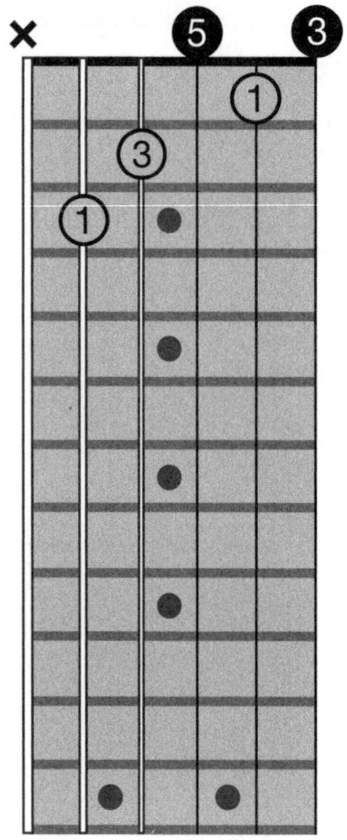

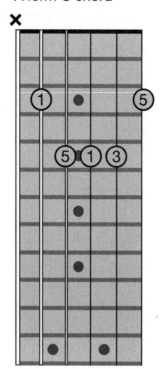

DIAGRAM 109:
A form C chord

DIAGRAM 110:
G form C chord

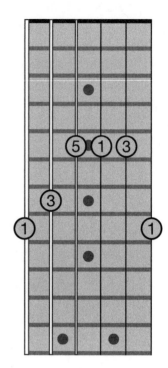

DIAGRAM 111:
E form C chord

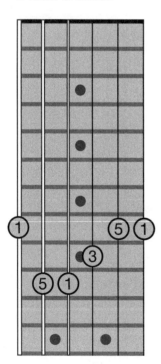

DIAGRAM 112:
D form C chord

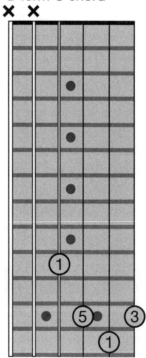

DIAGRAM 113:
E G# C# A and B root notes in the same area

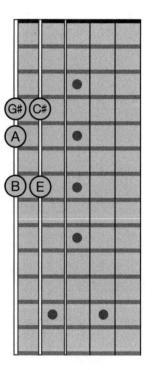

This _economy of movement_ can be seen in **Diagrams 114-118**. Finding the root notes in a different location **(Diagram 119)** will show you another option, as seen in **Diagrams 120-124**. As you can see, there are many ways to play any given chord progression. The choices are determined by the sound of the different chord voicings, the convenience of fingering, or a combination of both.

As you have probably noticed, we have omitted the F form from this approach. It may still be used as a separate form, but I think it is easier to think of it as the upper part of an E form chord.

DIAGRAM 114:
C form Emaj7

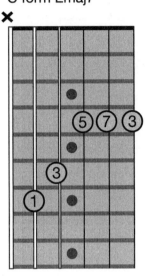

DIAGRAM 115:
E form G#min7

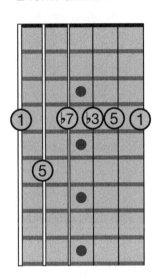

DIAGRAM 116:
A form C#min7

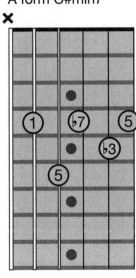

DIAGRAM 117:
E form A

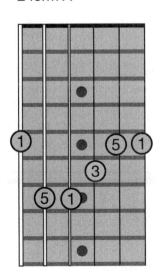

DIAGRAM 118:
G form B

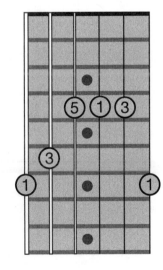

DIAGRAM 119:

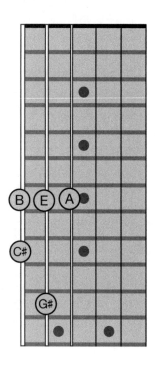

DIAGRAM 120:
A form Emaj7

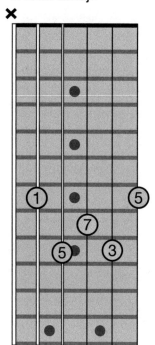

DIAGRAM 121:
C form G#min7

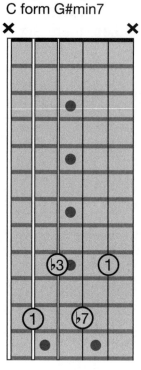

DIAGRAM 122:
E form C#min7

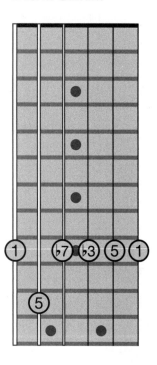

DIAGRAM 123:
D form A

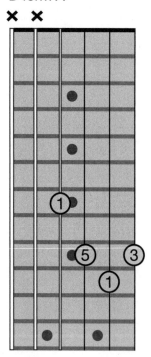

DIAGRAM 124:
E form B

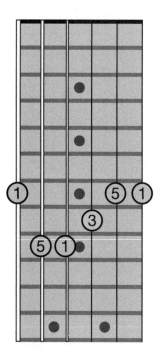

CHAPTER SEVEN - WORKBOOK

VISUALIZATION

Using the CAGED system, find an F chord in all areas on the fingerboard. Start with the E form and move through the rest of the forms (D C A G). Write them in on the following 5 neck blanks.

E form F chord   D form F chord   C form F chord   A form F chord   G form F chord

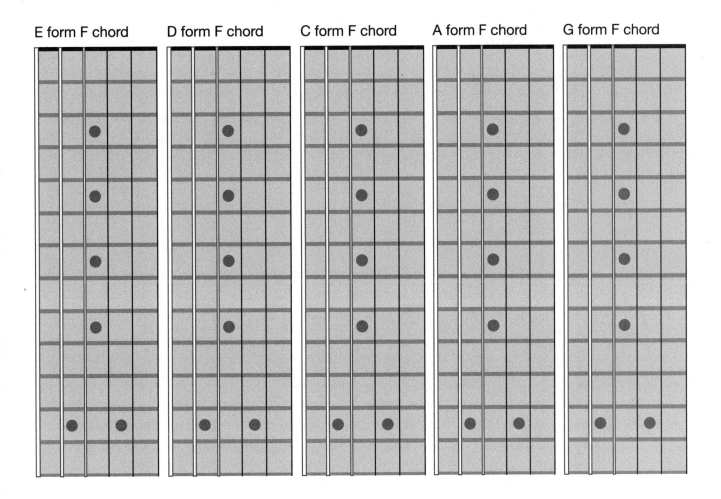

APPLICATION

On your instrument, find the following chord progression—C, F and G:

- In the first three frets

- From frets three to six

- From frets five to eight

- From frets seven to 10

- From frets 10 to 13

If this seems like a lot to you, it is! Find the progression in as many or few of these positions as you are able to without feeling overwhelmed. It is much more important to digest this information in small, manageable pieces than it is to push yourself to master everything at once.

CHAPTER EIGHT - PREFACE

It was 1961 and I was a sophomore at Sandia High School in Albuquerque. A couple of guitar players from the same school had heard me play and asked me if I would be interested in starting a band. They were both seniors and I thought it was cool that they wanted me, a lower-classman, to play with them.

The better player of the two had taken some lessons and knew some things that I didn't. One of the things that had the most impact on me was that linear shape for playing the pentatonic scale. This gave me more places to look for single-note riffs and a broader palette for my improvising.

They also were fans of the Ventures, and we set about learning to play instrumental songs. As it turned out, I had a better ear than either of these two. I ended up learning most of the new songs we wanted to play and showing them their parts. There was a little resentment towards me, being younger than they were, but we worked it out.

The other guitar players were Pete Webb and Robbie Cardin. We found a drummer named Larry Kuck. We were successful at finding gigs at local teen clubs and high school assemblies and parties. I was having more fun than at any previous time in my life. Being in a band in those days was way cool. There weren't many bands in high schools back then. Being in a band that played gigs was pretty special.

Things changed when Pete got a vice presidential appointment to the Air Force Academy and had to quit the band to prep for it. This left a hole in the band, which was filled by another guitar player named Jerry Shouse, who not only played good rhythm guitar but was also a good singer. This expanded what we could do; even though my heart was still in instrumental rock and roll, Jerry knew a bunch of Buddy Holly and Elvis Presley songs, which I liked. He also looked like Buddy Holly and sounded quite a bit like him, which later turned out to be a great advantage to us.

I was the lead guitarist in the band. Jerry sang, and he and Rob traded off playing rhythm guitar and bass. I had bought a cheap bass for them to use.

As we played more, the need for more and better equipment became obvious. I got my first real Fender amp at this time—a blonde Tremolux piggy-back amp, one of the first of its kind. The amp section was separate from the speaker cabinet, which had two 10" speakers in it. It had two channels, one normal channel and a lead channel that had an effect called tremolo, hence the name Tremolux. Reverb, a common effect in amps these days, hadn't been incorporated into Fender's amps at that time and was still only available as a separate unit.

The other guys had similar amps, but PA systems were not common back then, so we plugged the microphone into the second channel of one of the guitar amps and made do with that until we could find a small PA. The idea that we actually played gigs this way seems hardly possible in this day of large sound systems and digital technology.

All guitar amps back then were powered with vacuum tubes, a technology which is still preferred by most guitarists. The sound of the tubes just can't be equaled by even the most advanced digital technology. Guitar players are the primary users of tube technology,

The Tremolux was one of the first combo-style amplifiers of the era.

An early version of the Kingpins, with the guitar amplifiers doubling as the PA.

with the exception of high-end stereo equipment used by a few audiophiles, and some ham radio operators. We keep tube manufacturers in business!

My band, now called The Kingpins, spent the next two years playing local teen clubs in Albuquerque. The Wayside Inn and Little Beaver Town are two that come to mind. We also played some fraternity parties at UNM, high school functions, and some private events.

It was at one of these parties that we met a man who would offer us the opportunity to record at the Norman Petty Studios in Clovis, New Mexico— the studio where Buddy Holly and many other artists had recorded. His name was Bill Sego. He had gotten to know Norman Petty when he was in college at Eastern New Mexico University, also in Clovis. He had recorded at Petty's as vocal talent on a variety of projects and they had gotten quite close.

The Kingpins had a gig playing for a party that Bill had attended. He took a liking to the band, possibly because of Jerry's resemblance to Buddy Holly. After the gig, he approached us and

Norman Petty Studios in Clovis, NM—the recording studio where Buddy Holly cut his classic records, and where the Kingpins recorded their single for MGM.

said that he had a recording project that he wanted us to work on. He said that, if we could play the music to his satisfaction, he would arrange for us to go to Clovis and record it at Norman Petty Studios. Of course we jumped at the chance. What an opportunity!

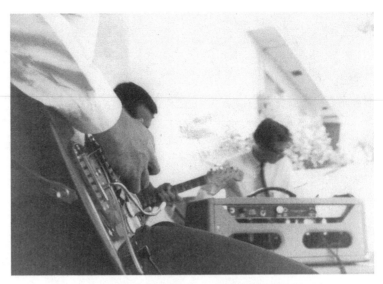

Steve, Jazzmaster and Tremolux onstage with the Kingpins at an outdoor event in Albuquerque, New Mexico.

The song that he wanted us to record was a rock and roll instrumental version of a Swedish folk song called "Hus Droma". I believe his wife was of Swedish heritage. He got a recording of the song to me and I set about learning it, arranging it, and teaching it to the rest of the guys. My good ear really paid off, and he was happy with what we had done. The single would be pressed to a two-sided, 45 rpm, 7-inch vinyl record. This meant we could record something of our own to put on the flip side. I had an instrumental song that I had written and it was decided that we would use it. Surf music was a happening thing at the time, so we called it "94 Second Surf,"seeing as the song was only a minute and 34 seconds long.

Steve playing his Jazzmaster during the early Kingpins days.
The Tremolux is visible in the bottom left, and the original tweed guitar case is in the bottom right.

87

*Both "Rod Hot Rod" and "94 Second Surf" appear on this compilation of Norman Petty's recordings from the era.
As a matter of diplomacy, both Norman's name ("Door Banger") and Steve's name ("94 Second Surf") are used for the single.
However, the female vocals are conspicuously absent.*

Both songs went through some changes. Norman, at his sole discretion, decided to rename the songs and add some female vocals. "Hus Droma" became "Rod Hot Rod" and "94 Second Surf" became "Door Banger". I have no idea what the thought process was behind these changes, but he was Norman Petty and his track record preceded him. Not only had Buddy Holly found his fame under Norman's guidance, but a well-known instrumental group, the Fireballs, had also recorded there and had two Top 40 hits.

Our hopes were that he could do the same for us. He shopped the record around and the Manhattan-based MGM records picked it up, with my original song as the A side! The song got quite bit of local airplay, being released on Bill Sego's Larse label. That year was a great year, cruising all the drive-ins while our song was played on the radio.

The local, pre-MGM pressing of the Kingpins' first and only single.

The single was still called "94 Second Surf" at that time. The name change and vocal additions were made as a part of Norman's attempts to generate major label interest. The song has since been included in 2 or 3 compilations of surf music and other music recorded at Norman Petty's studio. The general consensus is that the original version, prior to the added vocals, is the preferred version. A while ago it had even achieved collectible status, and some years later another band released a cover of it, under the original title.

Things were looking pretty good for us until late 1963. Just about the time that release dates were being set, President Kennedy was assassinated and business in New York shut down. Our single was put on hold and, just when the industry got rolling again, the second misfortune occurred. This misfortune was called the British Invasion: the Beatles arrived in early 1964, and instrumental rock and roll virtually ceased to exist.

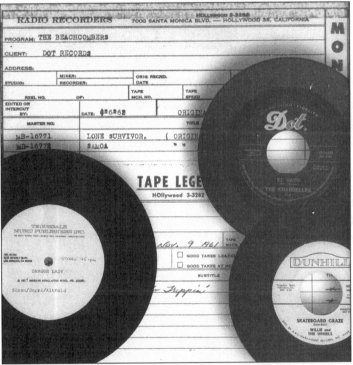

A compilation of surf and hot rod music that features the original version of
'94 Second Surf' surfaced in the United States in the mid-1990s.
It appears that the only recordings of the 'modified' version
are the original 7-inch LPs that MGM distributed in Japan.

MGM stopped the plan to release our single in this country. It was, however, released in Japan, where instrumental rock and roll was still popular. It sold fairly well overseas but was never released in the States.

So close, but not close enough. Oh well. On with the pursuit of knowledge on the instrument.

CHAPTER EIGHT - MORE ABOUT CHORDS

When I was 17, someone gave me a book called *Leed's Guitar Chord Dictionary*. It claimed to contain diagrams for over 2,400 chords. I was overwhelmed. How on earth could I possibly get to know all of these chords and find them without constantly referring to the dictionary? Even with a good memory and an even better ear, this seemed unattainable.

By now, you have seen that memorizing things is a poor substitution for understanding them. Knowing what it takes to make a chord and how to find those components on your guitar has given you the power to build chords and to find these chords in several places. Even so, this hardly seems to approach that 2,400 chord figure. And it turns out, there are actually many more than that.

In the interest of expanding your vocabulary, it is time to learn a few more chord types. The chords that we have learned so far are built by playing every other note of a scale, using the 1, 3, 5 and 7. *There are also chords that use the 2, 4 and 6 from these same scales.*

The first of these chords are called <u>suspended</u> chords, or 'sus chords' for short. Suspended chords are chords in which the 3rd is replaced either by 4 (<u>sus4 chords</u>) or 2 (<u>sus2 chords</u>). If you encounter a chord that just says 'sus,' it is safe to assume that a sus4 is wanted, as it is the more common of the two.

Music and the terminology used to describe it are continually changing and evolving things. Some chords that are used commonly today didn't exist a few decades ago. The sus2 chords are a prime example of the way the language of music adapts to include new sounds.

THE TERMINOLOGY BEHIND SUSPENDED CHORDS

The term "suspended" was originally used to refer to the ½ step movement between two chords whose resolution was delayed. A simple example is what happens when moving from an open G chord to an open D chord. The octave note of the G chord, found on the high E string, moves down 1/2 step into the 3rd of the D chord, F#. This is an example of <u>voice leading</u>, the way the notes in one chord move into the notes in the following chord. This <u>resolution</u> into the D chord can be delayed—or suspended—by leaving the G note in place. The G note then becomes the 4 of the Dsus4 chord.

Here is where the logic gets a bit fuzzy. Without understanding the term 'resolution' as discussed, it's not too far a stretch to define suspension as follows: If replacing the 3 with a 4 is called a sus4 chord, then replacing the 3 with a 2 could be called a sus2 chord, even though there is no ½ step resolution to justify the use of the term "sus". This mis-applied logic has led us to a new group of chords, the "sus2" chords. Maybe this is too much information, but I find the logic behind chord terminology to be fascinating.

Any of the chords we have learned can be changed to sus4 chords by replacing the 3 (or b3) with 4. Any chord can become a sus2 chord by replacing the 3 (or b3) with a 2. This expands our chord vocabulary considerably.

You will notice that sus4 and minor sus4 chords look the same. A chord is called a minor sus4 chord in reference to what the chord was before (or after) it was suspended.

Here are the resulting chord types:

Sus4	1	4	5	
minor sus4	1	4	5	(Called minsus4 when chord was originally minor)
7sus4	1	4	5	b7
min7sus4	1	4	5	b7
maj7sus4	1	4	5	7

Diagrams 125-129 show the open D chord changed to the sus4 chords.

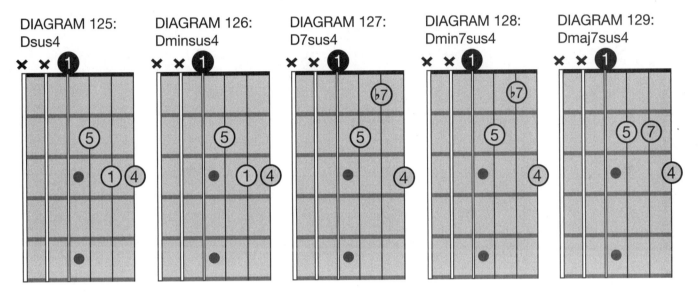

DIAGRAM 125:
Dsus4

DIAGRAM 126:
Dminsus4

DIAGRAM 127:
D7sus4

DIAGRAM 128:
Dmin7sus4

DIAGRAM 129:
Dmaj7sus4

Diagrams 130-134 show the open A chord changed to the sus4 chords.

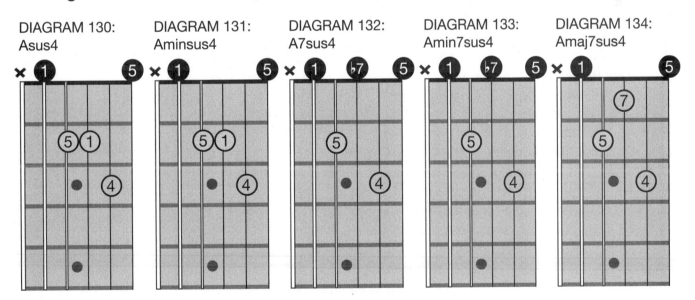

DIAGRAM 130:
Asus4

DIAGRAM 131:
Aminsus4

DIAGRAM 132:
A7sus4

DIAGRAM 133:
Amin7sus4

DIAGRAM 134:
Amaj7sus4

Diagrams 135-139 show the open E chord changed to the sus4 chords.

DIAGRAM 135:
Esus4

DIAGRAM 136:
Eminsus4

DIAGRAM 137:
E7sus4

DIAGRAM 138:
Emin7sus4

DIAGRAM 139:
Emaj7sus4

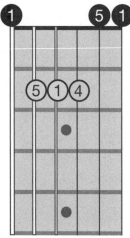 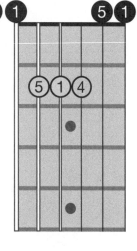 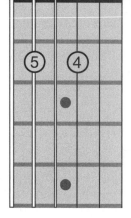 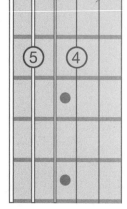 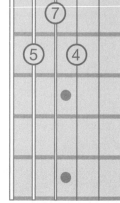

Sus2	1	2	5	
minor sus2	1	2	5	(Called minsus2 when the chord was originally minor)
7sus2	1	2	5	b7
min7sus2	1	2	5	b7
maj7sus2	1	2	5	7

Diagrams 140-144 show the open D chord changed to the sus2 chords.

DIAGRAM 140:
Dsus2

DIAGRAM 141:
Dminsus2

DIAGRAM 142:
D7sus2

DIAGRAM 143:
Dmin7sus2

DIAGRAM 144:
Dmaj7sus2

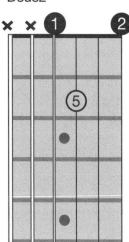 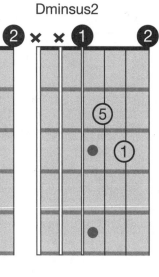 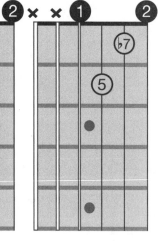 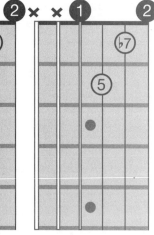

Diagrams 145-149 show the open A chord changed to the sus2 chords.

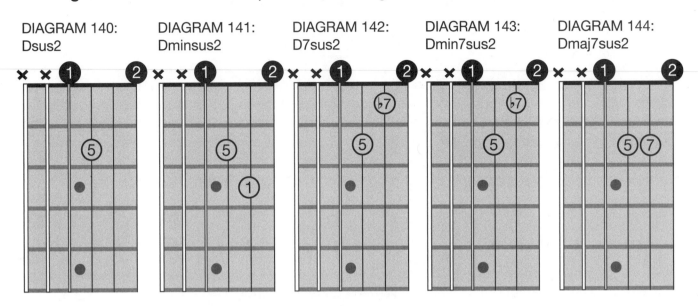

DIAGRAM 140:
Dsus2

DIAGRAM 141:
Dminsus2

DIAGRAM 142:
D7sus2

DIAGRAM 143:
Dmin7sus2

DIAGRAM 144:
Dmaj7sus2

The open E chord cannot be changed to a sus2 chord because the 3 cannot be lowered a whole step.

Any of the bar chord forms can be changed to sus chords through this same process. There are too many chords to diagram them all, but at this point you should know enough to be able to find them on your own.

As an example of the evolutionary aspect of music and the attempts to find terminology to describe our sonic language as it grows, the first time that I ever heard a maj7sus chord was in one of Steely Dan's songs, even they didn't know what to call it themselves. At the time, the band referred to these chords as 'Mu majors.' Since then, the maj7sus chord has become more common and was eventually absorbed into the 'sus chord' family as a result.

HOW MANY CHORDS CAN YOU FIND?

Up to this point, we have only been dealing with 5 chord types: major, minor, 7th, minor 7 and major 7. Adding these 10 new 'sus' chord types gives us a total of 15. Each chord can be played using any of the 12 notes of the chromatic scale as the root note. 12 root notes x 15 chord types = 180 chords.

Each of these chords can be played in any of the 6 chord forms we know (E, A, D, G, C and F). 180 chords x the 6 different chord forms = 1,080 chords.

We are getting closer to being able to find the 2,400 chords from *Leed's Guitar Dictionary* without having to memorize them individually. There are many, many more chord types yet to come.

CHAPTER EIGHT - WORKBOOK

APPLICATION

As we discussed, the introduction of suspended chords radically increases the number of chord types available to you. Sus chords can be used because of the different sound that they have. They can also be used to embellish chord progressions that are usually played using the chord types we already know.

For example, here is a simple chord progression using open A and D chords:

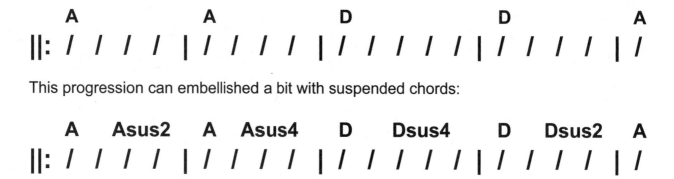

This progression can embellished a bit with suspended chords:

Rather than give you more examples at this time, I would like you to take other chord progressions that you know and experiment by using the sus chords to add different sounds to them. Experiment and see what you can create.

CHAPTER NINE - PREFACE

After the letdown of our near success with '94 Second Surf', the Kingpins drifted apart. I started playing with another local group, Lindy and the Lavells. The band was led by Lindy Blaskey. Blaskey was a good businessman and very good at promoting his and two other local bands, the Viscount V and the Striders. All three groups released records locally, each recorded at John Wagner Studios. John Wagner was from Clovis and had gained recording experience at Norman Petty's with his own band, the 5 Counts, before relocating to Albuquerque. He spent some time playing with the Lavells before opening his own studio. John Wagner Studios has been the mainstay in music and commercial recording in New Mexico for the last 40+ years.

AT RECORDING SESSION: Lindy and the LaVells join John Wagner (left) in his studio to listen to the tape of their latest record, "Papa-Omm-Mow-Mow." The LaVells are (from left in rear) Chuck Buckley, Danny Valdez, leader Lindy Blaskey and Steve Maase. (Staff photo)

Lindy Blaskey and the Lavells (misspelled "LaVells" by local press at the time) achieved some regional notoriety but never broke onto the national circuit. Like '94 Second Surf,' several of their singles have achieved 'collectible' status among aficionados of garage and surf music.

I played with Lindy and the Lavells off and on for a few years, but wasn't feeling fulfilled as a sideman. As I said, Blaskey was a shrewd businessman and paid all of his sidemen Union scale (which was very low), no matter how much the band was paid. He kept the majority of the band's earnings for himself. His business acumen served him well, and he went on to a career as an A&R man for a major record label.

Steve, remarkably self-effacing, caught in a rare smile during a press photo shoot shortly after the Kingpins disbanded.

I formed a band of my own, the Sunday Funnies. (My ability to name bands has never been my forte.) This band included keyboard player Carl Manfredi, bassist Mike Brown, singer Mickey Willins, drummer Les Bigbie and myself. We played primarily Top 40 music from the British Invasion—the Beatles, The Rolling Stones, the Animals, and so on. The band was fairly successful; we played gigs at the University of New Mexico, located in downtown Albuquerque, and at other colleges around the state. We also played at a local show club, Vena's Roaring 20's, and a few other clubs that have long since gone. We never did any recording, but we had a lot of fun. The band eventually faded into obscurity.

Around this time, I met my first wife and decided that I needed to find a way to be more financially stable. I was fortunate to be offered a job as a salesman at a local music store,

Sunday Funnies Flip Wigs in Top Tempo

By MAUREEN MOSIER

Wigs and falls have only added to the humor of the Sunday Funnies!

These funnies aren't the ones you read each weekend—these funnies are the five-member rock band, "The Sunday Funnies."

"We don't have a leader," says Mickey Willins, lead singer, adding "we all work together and do our own things."

Providing the accompaniment so Mickey has something to sing to are Mike Brown, bass guitar player; Les Bigby, drummer; Steve Maase, lead guitarist; and Carl Manfredi, organist and piano player.

The wigs and falls comment involves a bit of recent department store humor when Carl and Mickey sent customers into hysterics and stares by doning samples of the hair pieces.

All five admit they are a bit on the clownish side, except Steve, who is considered the group's quiet member.

All are previous band members who joined together last January.

"We all respected one another as fellow musicians and decided to join our music abilities and experience to see what we could come up with as a band," Mickey said.

Then came a frantic search for a name.

"Everyone had their pet names, but we finally decided on the Sunday Funnies, because it was unusual and original. That's what we wanted," Mickey said.

The group plans and hopes to cut their first record in the near future. They are currently working on an original composition, "Things I need," but first would "like to play round with different ones to come up with an original and commercial sound."

SUNDAY FUNNIES? No, these aren't the funnies you read in the newspapers, these Sunday Funnies are musicians. Front row Funnies are Mickey Willins and Carl Manfredi. Back row Funnies are Mike Brown, Steve Maase, and Les Bigbie.

The Sunday Funnies, as featured in the Albuquerque Journal.

Riedling Music Co. This happened largely due to my acquaintance, as a customer, with two other salesmen at the store—Art Bachman and Clyde Hankins (the guy that sold me my Jazzmaster a few years back). Both of these guys were guitarists, mostly into jazz players like Johnny Smith, Jimmie Rainey, Kenny Burrell, Barney Kessel, Joe Pass, and George Van Eps (the man credited with bringing the 7-string guitar into contemporary awareness long before it became a popular instrument in heavy metal). This music had a complexity that was new to my still-developing ears.

What a great job! I was finally in a situation where I could learn more about guitars and the related gear, and could get to know more players while I was at it—a job working with other guitar players who were better than I, guitarists that I could learn new things from.

The job had some other 'perks' as well: One day not long after I started at Riedling's, The Who were scheduled to play at the Civic Auditorium in downtown Albuquerque. A man who must have been their road manager came into the store and said he needed to find a couple of used Fender Stratocasters for the show that night, guitars that Pete Townsend would plan to smash onstage. As guilty as I felt about sending them to such an end, I found the manager two used Strats. He paid $250 each for the guitars. I shudder to think what two 1960's Strats would be worth in today's market.

Having a close brush with The Who was memorable to be sure, but the real reward of my time at Riedling's was my relationship with Clyde.

Clyde Hankins was a true guitar fanatic. He loved the instrument, and he also loved to teach. In fact, when he lived in Lubbock, Texas, one of his students was Buddy Holly! So he was familiar with rock and roll, but his real love was jazz guitar.

Whenever things at the store were slow, Art and Clyde would sit down and play jazz tunes together. This music was way over my head, but there was something about it that resonated within me. The first thing that I learned from Art and Clyde was how much I didn't know. Although my ear had taught me a lot and I had picked up bits of theory here and there, my limited knowledge of how music really worked became more obvious as I watched these guys play.

Clyde could see my interest in what they were playing and, when there were no customers in the store, he would show me how to play chords behind him on some of these more-common jazz tunes, known as 'jazz standards'. In the process of learning these songs I learned a bunch of new chords, many of which couldn't be found in that chord dictionary. The only problem was that, while Clyde would tell me the names of the chords (13th chords, 7b5b9, etc.), I was still just memorizing chord shapes and trying attach the correct name to them. More than ever I felt the need to develop a greater understanding of the theory behind it all.

I was still playing in rock and roll bands all this time, something that I have continued to do through most of my playing career. Rock and roll remained my first love as a guitarist, but my curiosity and desire to learn new things continued to grow. It was at about this time that I became acquainted with what has become my favorite word in the English language: **WHY**. It was no longer enough to just accept what my ear told me would work. I needed to know **WHY** things worked, and also why some things *didn't* work.

I had taken a theory class in high school. It was not a part of the regular curriculum, and was taught by the school's chorus teacher. I was glad to have the opportunity to take the class, but it was taught from the perspective of the piano. This is fairly common, because the piano still serves as the basis for comparison for most other instrumentalists; if you play the saxophone or the flute, for instance, odds are you will learn about music theory from looking at a piano keyboard.

I learned a bit about composition on the keyboard, but had no direct way of transferring this knowledge to my guitar. The only books that I could find on music theory were also written for keyboard, and these didn't transfer to the guitar very well at all. What was I to do?

I had a very basic knowledge of chord construction and had figured out how to see this information on the guitar. But everything I figured out seemed to bring up several other questions: Why do some chords fit together while others don't? Where do all these jazz chords come from? How could I improvise over these more complex chord progressions? And on, and on, and on.

The door into this particular room was opened by Bill Westbrook, the piano salesman at Riedling Music. Bill was also an accomplished jazz sax player, and I got to know him better at a few jam sessions. The guys from the store got together to play every once in a while and at times they needed a bass player when their regular guy couldn't make it. I sat in as a limited but willing sub.

I guess Bill was very aware of my limitations as a bass player (and guitar player), and during slow times at the store he took me aside and began to show me some of the technical aspects of music theory.

Rock Legend Followed Jazz Guitarist's Lead

By Bob Groves
JOURNAL ARTS WRITER

Meet the man who sold the late, great Buddy Holly his first Stratocaster, the pink Cadillac of electric guitars.

Though he showed Holly how to play a number of chords on various occasions, Albuquerque jazz guitarist Clyde Hankins insists he was not officially Holly's guitar teacher. Hankins also claims to have first told Holly about Norman Petty, the producer who launched Buddy Holly and the Crickets from his small recording studio in Clovis.

"I'm not a man who blows (brags), but Buddy just enjoyed hearing me play. He never asked me to show him how to play, just some advice on chords."

Actually Hankins — who was then, is now and always will be strictly a *jazz* guitarist — liked Holly immensely, but wasn't all that impressed when he first met him.

During the '50s, Hankins was working for Adair Music Co. on Avenue K in Lubbock, Texas, and playing guitar several days a week on Lubbock's only television station. One day in 1955, three kids about 20 years old came into the store with questions about guitars. The trio struck Hankins as being a tad on the hillbilly side. One of them was bare foot.

They were just three nice kids who turned out to be Buddy Holly and his two earliest sidemen, Larry Welborn and Bob Montgomery. (Later musician friends who made up Holly's group, the Crickets, at different times were Jerry Allison, Niki Sullivan, Joe Mauldin and Sonny Curtis. Curtis eventually worked as a guitar salesman with Hankins.) In his brief career, Buddy Holly put his own stamp on rockabilly music with a long string of hits such as "That'll Be the Day," "Maybe Baby," "Peggy Sue," "Not Fade Away," "Everyday" and "Oh Boy!"

"I'm not putting anybody down. It's just that they were playing a totally different kind of music," said Hankins recently at the Bob Farley Music Center, 3707 Eubank NE, where he is now a retired, part-time guitar salesman and teacher.

Hankins, who turns 67 today, performs locally with the Steve Gary Quartet. He has been playing guitar professionally since he was 13. Thirty years ago he copyrighted his own guitar chording method, which he has used in teaching.

"I thought rock 'n' roll was nothing. I didn't see anything there, and I had one of the top rock stars right there in the store several times. I was not impressed at all.

"But I *loved* the guy. He was a quiet, clean-cut super guy, a very religious young man, very quiet, very modest."

Around this time, Hankins

Clyde Hankins

JOURNAL PHOTO / MARK POULSEN

Hankins was photographed in 1942 at New York's Lincoln Hotel.

also worked with Petty, whose Clovis studio was as renowned in rockabilly circles as was Sam Phillips' Sun Records in Memphis. Petty produced a Hankins album of jazz standard tunes with George Atwood, another Holly musician, on bass.

Over the next couple of years Holly dropped in on Hankins a number of times, not for a guitar lesson as such, but for help on figuring out a particular chord change in a particular song. When Holly came by one day to buy some instruments and found that Hankins was working temporarily in Dallas, he got on the phone.

"Holly called me in Dallas and said, 'I want to buy from you.' He bought his Stratocaster guitar and a Fender amplifier, and a Fender bass and pro amp. He sent a check and we put them on the bus."

After a short while, Hankins returned to Lubbock. He last saw Holly about a week or so before he was killed, along with the Big Bopper and Ritchie Valens, in a small plane crash in Iowa Feb. 2, 1959. Holly was 22.

"Holly came out in his new Cadillac to our house for lunch and spent the day with my wife and I. Even then I didn't know

he was the biggest thing in rock 'n' roll at the time. He admired my music. He brought his guitars out for an adjustment and spent about four hours with us. We just talked music and adjusted his guitars and put on a couple sets of new strings."

Holly went back to New York City where he was pursuing a solo career and where he lived with his wife, Maria Elena. Against his better judgment, he decided to go on one more tour. Hankins heard the news of Holly's death and attended the closed-casket funeral.

Hankins admired rock guitarists such as Jimi Hendrix and Eric Clapton for their iconoclastic techniques and their influence on rock 'n' roll, but his real heroes were jazz guitarists from Charlie Christian, George Barnes, Barney Kessel and Herb Ellis to Joe Pass, Wes Montgomery and, above all, George Van Epps.

Hankins, whose father was a cowboy and country fiddler, was born in Hansford, Texas, near Amarillo. When he was 8, his family moved to San Diego. At 13, he volunteered his services

MORE: See ROCK on PAGE E8

Stratocaster's Still the Pick Of the Pickers

By Nathan Cobb
BOSTON GLOBE

FULLERTON, Calif. — It is ever so fitting that it has happened here, in a onetime orange grove located 35 miles southeast of downtown Los Angeles. Southern California, after all, likes to think of itself as America's post-World War II social volcano, spewing changes eastward over a grateful nation. Let us all give thanks for hot rods, hot tubs ....

And hot guitars. Especially the Fender Stratocaster, the foxy solid-body that first sounded its souped-up clarion in May 1954, and has gone on to become probably the most popular electric guitar ever made. The supersexy, ultrabright, maxi-California Strat.

It was invented as a country music guitar but swept along by the bright-lights childhood of rock 'n' roll. Used by all manner of well-remembered and long-forgotten pop musicians, from Jimi Hendrix to the Peanut Butter Conspiracy. The Strat: a name that has achieved generic status, like Xerox or Kleenex. A guitar to make your hair grab your collar.

"It is definitely the guitar of the '80s," says Tom Wheeler, editor of Guitar Player magazine. Which is a bit like calling the 1954 Corvette the 1985 Car of the Year. But the Stratocaster is so timeless, so classic that it has undergone only minor changes since its birth.

Its stiletto sound perseveres, as do its Candy Apple Red and Lake Placid Blue paint jobs. "Guitar players like it for its sound, but they also like it for its history," says Glenn Fitchette, manager of guitars and amplifiers at LaSalle Music, a Boston musical instrument store. "It's not a cult item, but it's got prestige value. It's got some kind of mystique."

Even though the Strat hasn't been altered much, guitar players tend to talk about the vintage models in the same tones used by auto collectors when crooning over a '42 Ford Wagon or a '55 Chevy Bel Air. Not unaware of that, Fender in 1981 began producing replicas of the treasured 1957 and 1962 Strats.

Still, many guitarists insist on remaining loyal to what they consider to be the real thing. One of them is Stuart Kimball, who plays in Face to Face, a Boston-based rock band, using a '60 Strat with a '57 neck. "That's the original sound," Kimball emphasized. "Everything else is a copy. And why have a copy if you can have the original?"

Here, in the former groves of Orange County,

JOURNAL PHOTOS

'70s Stratocaster sports rising-sun pick guard.

the huge and low-slung factory that houses Fender Musical Instruments displays a conspicuous For Sale sign. Inside are the dismembered production lines, the unused piles of Eastern hardrock maple and the abandoned employee gymnasium.

Sold last month by CBS Inc., its owner for 20 years, Fender is now in the hands of a group of investors headed by the company's president, William Schultz. It is looking for smaller quarters, although most of its production — including that of 11 of its 19 Stratocaster models — will soon move to Japan, where much of it has recently been taking place anyway. The Strat — currently yours for a suggested retail price of between $299 to $999, depending on the model — lives on.

MORE: See STRATOCASTER'S on PAGE E2

Steve and Buddy Holly had something in common besides Norman Petty—a musical mentor! Steve often credited Clyde as being his only real 'teacher' over the course of his career. The article on page left is included as a matter of interest: at its end is a brief mention of the Fender factory's sale to a group of investors who planned to move the factory overseas. This proved to be a pivotal and tumultuous point in the company's history, launching a rare period during which the models imported from Japan seemed by and large to be of a superior quality to the versions made at home.

Most musicians are exposed to at least the basics of music theory and learn to read as a part of their initiation into the instrument. Guitar players, with the exception of some well-trained classical players, tend not to learn this way.

Guitar has mostly been taught as an oral tradition. Most guitarists learn the instrument by sitting down with other players who are willing to share what they know. Even when a student develops a relationship with a teacher, this interaction is usually the basis of that relationship.

When I take on a student, the first thing I ask is, "What do you want to be able to play?" Then I ask: "What got you interested in the guitar? What music do you listen to?" From there, I start by showing them how to play what they want to learn.

In other words, for guitarists, music theory is taught on a need-to-know basis. I show my students what they need to know to become better players and be able to play what they are drawn to, but I don't make the complexities of theory a prerequisite to learning to play. We tackle theory when (and if) the student recognizes the need to know, after they become acquainted with my favorite word—**WHY**.

I had reached this point a while before Bill Westbrook offered to explain things to me. So I was ready and hungry for the knowledge he had to offer. Bill was able to show me the biggest missing piece in my understanding: the concept of keys. Keys turned out to be the basis of chord-scale relationships and the thing that would answer many of the questions that I had.

CHAPTER NINE - KEYS, AN INTRODUCTION

Up to this point, I had looked at chords as being separate entities. I had no real understanding of how or why they could be used and let my ear make most of the choices for me.

But I had begun to have some pressing questions about the 'bigger picture' of the music I was making: How did chords really fit together? Why were some chords used frequently in progressions? Why were some chords played as 7th chords, and others as major 7 or minor 7 chords? The answer to these and many more questions lay in the concept of <u>keys</u>.

The term "key" is often misunderstood and, as a result, misused. Some people refer to the key of a song as determined by the first chord in a song, the last chord in a song, or the chord used most frequently in a song. Some think that a progression using minor chords is always in a minor key, or that the key signature of a song determines the key for the entire piece. While these things may occasionally be true, they are not a reliable way of determining the key of a song.

So, what does the term 'key' really mean?

Bill had a way of showing me about keys on a piano keyboard that I was able to understand and make use of on the guitar. These concepts apply to any instrument but, as I mentioned, the guitar is often left out of the picture when it comes to discussing theory. So I was grateful to find Bill, and the following is my understanding of keys based on what he told me.

KEY = MAJOR SCALE

Simply put, the term 'key' means 'major scale'. If a song is in a key, the contents of the song are derived from the notes in the major scale of that key.

If a song is in the key of C, the melodic and chordal content of that song are derived from the notes in the C major scale. If melody or chords occur that are not found in that scale, there has usually been a change of key. To help you see how this works, the first thing that we'll do is figure out what basic chords can be made using only the notes of the major scale.

To do this, let's build a four-note chord starting from each note in the major scale. This process is called <u>harmonizing the major scale</u>.

As you know, chords are made by playing every other note of a scale. This is to maintain distance between the notes to avoid dissonance. We'll start this with the key of C, but the results will apply to *all keys*. The following scale is written over two octaves to make the process easier to see.

C D E F G A B C D E F G A B C

1 $_1$ 2 $_1$ 3 $_½$ 4 $_1$ 5 $_1$ 6 $_1$ 7 $_½$ $8^{(1)}$ 2 $_1$ 3 $_½$ 4 $_1$ 5 $_1$ 6 $_1$ 7 $_½$ $8^{(1)}$

Looking at the 'harmonized major scale' chart below, the first thing you can see is what the root notes of the chords are. But all those intervals in the chart don't mean much yet, with the exception of the chord built on the first note of the key. You can see that this chord is a major 7 chord. We can use this chord to create a formula that will help you figure out the other chords in the key.

THE HARMONIZED MAJOR SCALE

C -	1	2 steps	3	1½ steps	5	2 steps	7
D -	2	1½	4	2	6	1½	8
E -	3	1½	5	2	7	1½	2
F -	4	2	6	1½	8	2	3
G -	5	2	7	1½	2	1½	4
A -	6	1½	1	2	3	1½	5
B -	7	1½	2	1½	4	2	6

Looking at the major 7 chord in terms of the distances between the notes will give us a formula for all major 7 chords:

Major 7 chord: 1   2   3   1½   5   2   7

Any of the chords in the harmonized major scale that conform to this formula are major 7 chords.

Flatting the 7 in this chord, as we know, creates a 7th chord. The b7 in the chord changes the formula. The formula for 7th chords is:

7th chord: 1   2   3   1½   5   1½   b7

Chords in the harmonized scale that conform to this formula are 7th chords.

A minor 7 chord is made by lowering the 3 and the 7, resulting in the following formula:

Minor 7 chord: 1   1½   b3   2   5   1½   b7

Chords following this formula will be minor 7 chords.

Comparing the chords in the harmonized major scale to these formulas will tell you what chord types occur in which positions in the key.

There is, however, one chord in the key that doesn't fit any of these formulas. The chord built on the 7th degree of the scale is different. The formula of this chord is one we haven't encountered before. The whole steps and ½ steps create a <u>min7b5 chord</u>. It might help to look at the minor 7 chord formula and see how replacing 5 with b5 changes the formula:

Min7b5 chord: 1   1½   b3   1½   b5   2   b7

As you compare the chords in the harmonized major scale, the results will be as follows. To keep us from getting the degrees of the scale—or intervals—confused, we refer to the numbered chords in a key with Roman numerals:

I	II	III	IV	V	VI	VII
maj7	min7	min7	maj7	7th	min7	min7^{b5}

As I am sure you are aware, not all progressions use four-note chords. Many songs are played using triads. By leaving off the 4th note of the chords in the harmonized major scale, we can see what the triads are in any key:

I	II	III	IV	V	VI	VII
major	minor	minor	major	major	minor	diminished

(The <u>diminished triad</u> is played using 1, b3 and b5. We will discuss diminished chords and diminished 7th chords a bit later.)

The important thing to realize at this point is that *all keys are equal within themselves*: While the root notes of the chords are going to be different, (as determined by the notes in the scale of the key), the chord types built on those notes remain consistent. I chords are always major triads or major 7 chords, II chords are always minor or minor 7, and so on.

One of the advantages to thinking of progressions in terms of the numbered relationship of the chords to the key is <u>transposing</u>, or moving any chord progression to a different key. Being able to take a song that is written or played in one key and change it to another key is often necessary. It allows you to put the song in a key that is better for a vocalist, or a key that lays better for a particular instrument. As an example of the second situation, a lot of standard tunes were written in flat keys (Bb, Eb, Ab, etc.). These keys don't always work well for guitar players. Moving a song from the key of Eb to the key of E or G—a key more accessible to a guitarist—can make the difference in how achievable a song is.

If you can analyze a song and number the chords, the Roman numerals are going to have the same relationship to the new key. For example: The chord progression Eb, Cmin7, Fmin7, Bb7 can be easily transposed to another key if you see the progression as I, VI, II, V from the key of Eb.

Once you see these relationships as universal, moving the progression to the key of G becomes easy:

	I	VI	II	V
<u>In Eb:</u>	Eb	Cmin7	Fmin7	Bb7
<u>Transposed to the key of G:</u>	G	Emin7	Amin7	D7
<u>Transposed to the key of E:</u>	E	C#min7	F#min7	B7

Being able to think of progressions in terms of their parent key will give you some ease in improvising or creating melodies. As we discussed when we took our first look at chord-scale relationships, playing over chord changes could involve playing within the scale of each chord, and then changing scales as the chords change. This approach is a valid way to play through a chord progression, but our knowledge of keys can show us another, easier approach.

We know that, if they are in the same key, all of the chords in a progression share a common point of origin: the scale of the key. If you can determine what key a song is in, the scale of the key is one place to look for ideas. We'll discuss other approaches as we learn about modes a bit later. For now, the current approach is simple and valid, and should work as long as your analysis of the key is correct.

So, how do you go about figuring out what key a song is in? It might help to look at songs as puzzles waiting to be explored. Some clues for solving these puzzles are:

1. The type of chords being played.
2. The relationship of the chords to each other.

For example, let's look at a progression that begins with an Amin7 chord. The song is not necessarily in Amin. As you can see, minor 7 chords occur as either the II, III or VI chord of a key. The key of A minor, Amin7 is just one of the minor 7 chords that can occur within the harmonized major scale.

I	II	III	IV	V	VI	VII
maj7	min7	min7	maj7	7th	min7	min7b5

The Amin7 chord by itself doesn't tell us what key we are in, but it does narrow it down to one of three possibilities:

1. Amin7 could be the II chord in the key of G.
2. Amin7 could be the III chord in the key of F.
3. Amin7 could be the VI chord in the key of C.

In order to solve this puzzle, we need to look further into the chord progression. Let's say that the next chord in the progression is a D7 chord. While minor 7 chords are found in three positions in a key, 7th chords are found only as V chords in a key. If D is V, what is I?

Let's explore this further. Find a D note on your A string. Playing this as it occurs in an E form chord, you can see that D is the 5th of G. (Using the shapes of intervals as they are seen in the major scale can help you identify interval relationships. This can be easier and more accurate than counting through scale degrees. Look at the octave of an E form major scale and learn the shapes of 1 and 2, 1 and 3, 1 and 4 and so on.)

1. The D7 chord is the V chord of the key of G.
2. Is there an Amin7 chord in the Key of G? Yes. Amin7 is found in the key of G as the II chord.

The progression Amin7 to D7 is a II to V progression in the key of G. To verify your results, try improvising over the chords using the notes in the G major scale. You may have to experiment a bit to find workable ideas, but the scale will fit!

If the Amin7 chord were followed by a Bb chord instead of a D7, the key would be different. Major triads are found as the I, IV or V chords of a key. The chord itself doesn't help much, but the fact that the root notes of the two chords are ½ step apart will tell us what we need to know. The ½ steps in the major scale are found between 3 and 4, and between 7 and 8(1). Of these two options, a minor 7 chord with a major chord ½ step above it only occurs in the positions of III and IV in a key. This means that Amin7 and Bb *have* to be III and IV of the key of F. Try playing an F major scale over these chords. It will work!

Let's look at another example—the chord progression Amin7, Dmin7, Amin7, Emin7. In this progression, each chord could be either a II chord, III chord or a VI chord. Since minor 7 chords are found in these three positions, one way to determine the key would be to find the three keys that each minor 7 chord could be found in and see what key, if any, they have in common.

But this is *hard!* Thankfully, there's a shortcut.

If you look at where the minor 7 chords occur in the key, you'll notice that two of them— the II and III chords—are a whole step apart. Now look at the progression and see if there are two minor 7 chords a whole step apart. They don't need to be adjacent to each other in the progression; they just need to be there.

The Dmin7 and Emin7 chords are one step apart. This makes them II and III. If Dmin7 is II, the I must be C. The progression is therefore VI, II, VI, III from the key of C. Try playing the C major scale over the progression to be sure.

When trying to determine what key a chord progression is in, the following guidelines will be quite helpful:

- 7th chords occur as V only.
- Two minor or minor 7 chords a whole step apart occur as II and III.
- Two major chords a whole step apart occur as IV and V.
- A minor (or minor 7) chord and a major (or major 7) chord a half step apart occur as III and IV.
- A major 7 chord with a minor 7 chord a whole step above it occur as I and II

The workbook section contains more examples (puzzles) for you to solve and some suggestions to help you with this process.

THE RELATIVE MINOR CHORD

In our earlier exploration of the pentatonic scale, we talked about its use as the relative minor scale of a major chord 1½ steps above. Now that we know about key/chord relationships, let's take a closer look at what this relative minor chord is.

As the name states, the relative minor chord is a minor or minor 7 chord that has a lot in common with a major chord—in this instance, the I chord of a key.

There are three minor 7 chords in a key. By looking at these chords as they occur in the harmonized scale, we can see their relationship to the I chord:

C maj7 -	**1**	2 steps	**3**	1½ steps	**5**	2 steps	**7**
D min7 -	**2**	1½	**4**	2	**6**	1½	**8**
E min7 -	**3**	1½	**5**	2	**7**	1½	**2**
A min7 -	**6**	1½	**1**	2	**3**	1½	**5**

In the key of C, the II chord, Dmin7, has one note in common with the I chord: the root note. The III chord, Emin7, has three notes in common with the I chord: the 3, 5 and 7.

The VI chord, Amin7, also has three notes in common with the Cmaj7 chord. These notes make up the major triad—1, 3 and 5. Having the major triad in common, the VI chord shows the closest relationship to the I chord.

The VI chord is the relative minor chord. This chord and its scale can be used as a *substitution scale* for the I chord.

This means the relative minor scale is another viable option for playing over a chord progression. The pentatonic scale is often not a complete enough scale to work well in all situations. The notes that are added to the minor 7 pentatonic scale as the relative minor of a key are **2 and b6**. This is the diatonic relative minor scale. You can see its relationship to the pentatonic scale in **Diagram 150**. We'll find out more about why this works at a later time, when we learn about modes.

DIAGRAM 150: Amin7 diatonic 'relative minor' scale

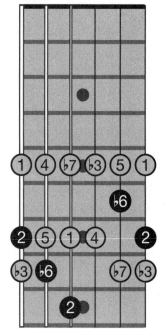

CHAPTER NINE - WORKBOOK

INFORMATION

LEVEL ONE

1. What does it mean if a song is in a 'key'?

_____

_____

_____

_____

2. There are three minor 7 chords in a key. Where do they occur?

_____

_____

_____

_____

3. There are two major 7 chords in a key. Where do they occur?

_____

_____

_____

_____

4. Where does the 7th chord occur?

_____

_____

_____

_____

5. What type of chord is built in the VII position of the harmonized major scale?

_____

_____

_____

_____

6. The VI chord is called the relative minor chord. Why?

_____

_____

_____

_____

INFORMATION

LEVEL TWO

In order to analyze chord progressions, you'll need to be able to see the relationship of notes to each other. For example, you'll need to be able to find what the III chord of a key is.

First, you need to know what note is the third note of the key. Then, you need to know what type of chord is built on that degree of the scale.

For example:

- The third note in the C scale is E.
- The chord built on the third note of the major scale is a minor 7 chord.
- The III chord of C is Emin7.

The relationship of notes to each other can be found by counting through scales, but the shapes of these note relationships can make this easier to accomplish. The following diagrams will show you the shapes of these intervals.

1 and 2   1 and 3   1 and 4

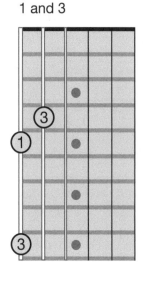

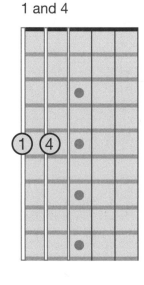

1 and 5   1 and 6   1 and 7   1 and 8 (1)

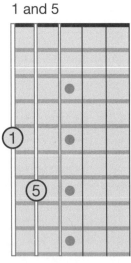

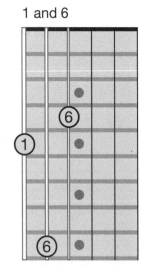

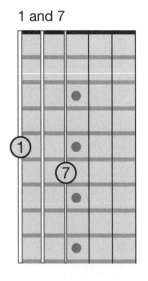

<u>Answer the following questions. Knowing the shapes of the intervals will help with this:</u>

- What is the 3rd of G? _____
- What is the 2nd of G? _____

- What is the 5th of F? _____
- What is the 5th of C? _____

- What is the 4th of Eb? _____
- What is the 4th of D? _____

- What is the 2nd of C#? _____
- What is the 3rd of F#? _____

- What is the 6th of A? _____
- What is the 7th of Bb? _____

- What is the 7th of F? _____
- What is the 6th of B? _____

<u>Answer the following questions:</u>

- G is the 3rd of what scale? _____
- G is the 2nd of what scale? _____

- F is the 5th of what scale? _____
- C is the 5th of what scale? _____

- Eb is the 4th of what scale? _____
- D is the 4th of what scale? _____

- C# is the 2nd of what scale? _____
- F is the 3rd of what scale? _____

- A is the 6th of what scale? _____
- A is the 7th of what scale? _____

- F is the 7th of what scale? _____
- B is the 6th of what scale? _____

Answer the following questions:

- What is the II chord of Bb? _____
- What is the IV chord of A? _____

- What is the VI chord of D? _____
- What is the VI chord of C? _____

- What is the IV chord of G? _____
- What is the VII chord of B? _____

- What is the III chord of Ab? _____
- What is the V chord of Eb? _____

- What is the VII chord of F? _____
- What is the II chord of C#? _____

- What is the V chord of Db? _____

APPLICATION

Some groupings of chords within keys occur more commonly than others. The most common of these are:

- I   IV   V
- I   V
- I   V   I
- I   V   IV   V
- I   VI   II   V

Being able to recognize these chord groupings will help you develop your ability to determine keys and key changes in songs.

Figure out the I IV V progression in the following keys: C, F, G, Bb, Eb, F#, D.

Then find the II V, II V I, I VI IV V, and I VI II V progressions in the same keys. It is probably best to start with the key of C and go through all the progressions in that key, then move to the key of F and do the same thing, gradually moving through all the progressions in all of the listed keys.

This is a *big* exercise. Take as long as you need to, getting used to the progressions one key at a time. It may help to start by first locating the root notes in the progression, then taking a second pass through the changes to build the chords from those root notes. You can find the root notes in any place on the fingerboard.

Remember that triads or seventh chords can be can be used, or a combination of both if you prefer.

For example, let's start with a I IV V progression in the key of C. Find the root notes starting with the C note on the A string. The root notes of IV and V are F and G, and can be found on the low E string. The progression can be played with triads: C, F and G. It can also be played as Cmaj7, Fmaj7 and G7. You can combine triads and seventh chords to play the progression as C, F and G7.

Try the II V, the II V I, and so on.

When you are ready to move on, find the root notes starting from the C on the low E string and F and G on the A string and go through the progressions in that area of the fingerboard.

As I said, this is a **BIG** exercise and it may take you a while to work through the whole thing. If necessary, take a key every few days—or a key a week—but be persistent. After you do the first key, the rest will get easier.

As you play these progressions, they should sound familiar. They are the basis for many songs. 'A version of the' I IV V progression is used in the Richie Valens song "La Bamba". The II V progression is the basis for the Santana song "Oye Como Va". There have been many songs from the 50's and 60's written using the I VI IV V progressions. Listen to the progressions as you play them and see if you can connect them to songs you have heard.

CHAPTER TEN - PREFACE

Rock and roll music has had diverse influences. Among the most prominent of these are the blues and R&B. Growing up in a middle class neighborhood in the Northeast Heights of Albuquerque, I wasn't exposed too much of these genres. For much of my early years as a guitar player, the blues was a missing influence.

My first exposure to the blues came through a high school friend, Noel Rozelle. He was an aspiring guitarist, and his father also played. On one occasion, I had gone to his house and we were playing some music when he asked me if I had ever heard of Freddie King. He pulled out an album, *Let's Hide Away and Dance Away with Freddie King*. The album was full of instrumental, blues-based songs like "Hideaway," "San-ho-zay," "The Stumble" and "Sen-Sa-Shun". These songs were covered by bands at that time, and are still played by blues enthusiasts.

This was just what I needed as my first exposure to the blues! As with the Ventures, vocal blues would probably not have been as intriguing to me at that time. Freddie King's music was perfect for me because I could hear every little thing that he was playing.

I immediately went out and bought the album and set about learning these songs and the nuances of this newfound style. I ended up learning most of the songs on that record and added some of them to my repertoire in various bands.

Learning to play Freddie King's music gave me my first foothold in the blues genre. From there, I developed a growing appreciation for its nuances, and over my lifetime I have learned a number of blues styles—from the music's roots in the Delta blues to Chicago blues, modern blues and beyond.

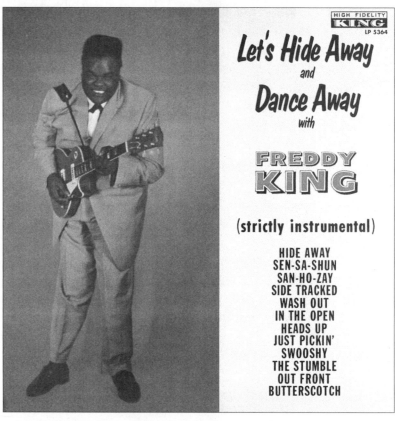

Freddy King is often described as one of the "Three Kings" of Blues guitar, along with B.B. King and Albert King. He tended to favor instrumental blues a bit more than the other two.

From early players like Robert Johnson up to the more contemporary players like Stevie Ray Vaughn and Joe Bonamassa and the jazz-influenced players like Robben Ford, the blues is as deep and varied as the people who play it.

This exposure to the blues made it easier for me to appreciate the music of groups from the British Invasion. This may sound strange, but American record companies didn't initially feel there was a market for music written and performed by black artists. As a result, some bluesmen had taken their music to England where there was a more receptive audience. Pop/rock groups from "across the pond" were responsible for taking this American musical form and bringing it back to this country as a part of rock and roll. Groups like Cream, Led Zeppelin and the Rolling Stones brought their blues-infused rock music to the American audience.

Ultimately, American artists like B.B. King, Albert King, Buddy Guy and, of course, Jimi Hendrix finally found wider acceptance in no small part due to these British bands.

As I went on to discover the music of jazz players like Kenny Burrell, I recognized the influence of blues in jazz. The blues, it turns out, is everywhere! Blues is a part of R&B and Gospel music. You can hear its influence in western swing and the improvisation in bluegrass. The blues has found its way into the more contemporary country music, has been at home in all styles of rock and roll, and is a profound part of any player's journey toward understanding the fundamentals of lead and rhythm guitar.

At the time, Jimi Hendrix's sound had just begun to change the world. His presence was so fresh, in fact, that an upcoming concert appearance was promoted through this modest handbill at Riedling's music, where Steve worked in retail alongside mentors Clyde Hankins and Bill Westbrook.

CHAPTER TEN - THE BLUES

Blues styles and techniques have found their way into many of the genres that are integral to the history of the guitar. Country players, folk players, rock players, jazz players—in fact, almost all guitar players—at times borrow from the musical form, technique, and feeling that we know as the blues. Just about every guitarist has at least *tried* to play the blues. Because of its far-reaching impact and its place as a common ground between guitarists, it is important to have a basic understanding of the genre and how it works.

Although the blues is not thought of as an intellectually-based musical idiom, its presence in this theory book is essential. While it is probable that the players in the roots of the blues had little or no knowledge of music theory, we can still use our understanding of chord scale relationships to learn about the genre as we begin to play it.

One crucial thing to remember about the blues is that it involves *improvising*. If you were to listen to a blues guitarist solo over the same song twice, you would hear something very different the second time around. While there may be some repeated themes, much of what you hear will be unique. It will only happen exactly the way it is happening in the moment that it is being played—this is improvising.

As I learned to play those Freddie King songs and other blues-based rock and roll songs as part of my personal journey toward understanding the guitar, I found that the minor 7 pentatonic scale was just about everywhere. It was the primary scale used for improvising and the basis for most guitar riffs in the genre. But, even though its presence was almost universal, I discovered some important variations to the pentatonic scale that were crucial to understanding how it works in blues.

As it stands, the minor 7 pentatonic scale actually *doesn't* work in all situations. There are some changes to be made to the scale that can allow it to work while staying within the blues idiom. But before we look at the scales used in playing the blues, we need to look at the basic chord progressions that make the blues what it is.

CHORDS IN THE BASIC BLUES

The first step toward understanding and making use of the blues idiom is to look at the basic blues progression. While it may seem simple at first glance, when we look deeper, it turns out the chords that make up the standard '12-bar blues' lead us to something more complex.

One of the things that typifies the blues is the use of 7th chords. While minor 7 chords appear in some blues songs, the most basic blues progressions use 7th chords almost exclusively. There are many different configurations of blues progressions, but the most common is the 'I IV V' progression.

As we learned in our study of keys, the four-note chords in any key occur in a specific order. I and IV are always major 7 chords, and the V chord is the *only* 7th chord in any key. The use of the terminology 'I IV V' in blues is used primarily because the root note of these 7th chords are the 1st, 4th and 5th notes in the scale of the 'key'. The fact that they are all 7th chords means that all three chords *cannot be* in the same key; even though their root notes may have this relationship, the arpeggios of the chords themselves tell a different story.

For example, a blues progression in the 'key of G' would use the following chords:

I	IV	V
G7	**C7**	**D7**

A blues progression in the 'key of A' would use the following chords:

I	IV	V
G7	**D7**	**E7**

Three separate 7th chords indicates that each blues progression actually occurs in three different keys! We'll take a closer look at this in a minute.

THE 12-BAR BLUES IN 'A'

In the <u>12-bar blues</u>, the term 'bar' is used to refer to a measure of music. This 12-measure, repeating form is probably the most commonly-used chord progression in the blues. It can, of course, be transposed to any key, but for now let's use the blues in 'A' as an example:

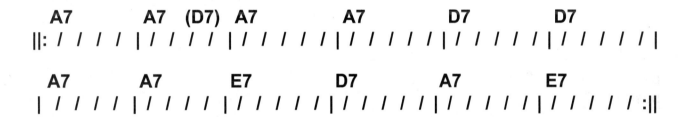

There are some variations to this form, the most common of which is a D7 chord played instead of the A7 in the 2nd measure. Another area that is often changed is the last measure (or two), referred to as the <u>turnaround</u>. This is a literal way of describing the measure (or measures) at the end of a repeated chord progression in order to 'turn it around' to the beginning.

One common 'turnaround' variation is:

A7   D7   A7   E7
| / / / / | / / / / |

THE SHUFFLE, OR TRIPLET, FEEL

While this progression is in 4/4 time, it is commonly played using ⅛ note <u>triplet</u> phrasing. In our 12-bar blues progression, each beat is divided into three ⅛ notes with the chords played on the first and third beats. This 'broken triplet' phrasing is referred to as a <u>'shuffle' feel</u>.

The chords played in each measure alternate between having the 1 and 5, and the 1 and 6 played in the lower part of each chord. Each measure would look like this:

```
 ||  / - /  / - /  / - /  / - /  ||
     5 - 5  6 - 6  5 - 5  6 - 6
     1 - 1  1 - 1  1 - 1  1 - 1
```

This rhythm pattern is 'plugged in' to every measure in the 12 bar blues progression, with the root note changing to fit the chords.

This brings up of the often-confusing discussion of time in music: In most of life, a ¼ note is divided into two notes called ⅛ notes. The concept of <u>triplets</u>, however, takes the time occupied by a ¼ note and divides it into three equal parts. This means that a measure of 4/4 time played in ⅛ note triplets would contain twelve ⅛ notes. This could also be referred to as 12/8 time. Both ways of describing the shuffle feel are correct—the terminology is basically a matter of personal preference.

When it comes to music, a traditional use of fractions won't always work. For instance, let's look at what happens when a measure of time is divided into 3 equal parts: The conventional approach would be to say the measure is divided into thirds. But, as with many things in music, our use of language is a bit unconventional. There are no ⅓ notes in music. Each of these notes would still be called a ¼ note. This time signature is called ¾ time. In other words, the top number in the fraction (3) indicates the number of beats in a measure, and the bottom number (4) indicates which kind of note is considered a 'beat.'

IS 'BLUES IN A' *REALLY* IN THE KEY OF A?

As previously mentioned, the fact that all three chords in the basic blues progression are 7th chords keeps us from looking at the chords as being in the same key. Based on our understanding of keys, referring to the 12-bar 'Blues in A' progression as being in the *key* of A is not really correct. As we found in the harmonized major scale, the 7th Chord is found only as the V chord of a key. This means that this 'Blues in A' is really not in the key of A at all. Here's why:

- If the A is a 7th chord, it would have to be the V chord of the key of D.
- The D7 chord would be found as the V chord of the key of G.
- The E7 chord is The V chord of the key of A.

Every chord in this progression is in a different key! So, while many look at the blues as being a 'simple' musical form, it can actually be quite harmonically complex.

When we talked previously about improvising over progressions in a key, we found that the scale of the key could be used over the progression. *In the blues, every time the chord changes, the key changes.* This means a different scale could be used over every chord! We'll figure out how to deal with this after we learn about the blues scale.

THE BLUES SCALE

Blues players have found many ways of playing over the 12-bar blues progression, from the basic, pentatonic-based minor blues scale to concepts that require an awareness of more complex chord-scale relationships. Let's start with the basic <u>blues scale</u>.

The blues scale is based on that powerful pentatonic scale that we learned about in Chapter 6. There are, however, some distinct differences between a pentatonic scale and what we will define as the 'blues scale'. The first of these differences is the addition of the b5 to the scale. This non-scale note—or '<u>blue note</u>'—is used as a chromatic (½ step) passing note between the 4 and 5 in the pentatonic scale. In other words, 'blue notes' are notes that are not really found in the scale of the chord but are used to slur into scale notes or to move chromatically between them.

While this scale is often referred to as being the blues scale, because of the b3 and b7 we will think of this as the minor 7 blues scale. This blues scale is shown in **Diagram 151** and the linear position of the scale is shown in **Diagram 152**. In the most basic blues, players use this scale to play over all three chords in the blues progression, even though not all the notes in the scale fit harmonically with all the notes in the scale fit harmonically with all the chords in their related keys.

Way back in Chapter 5, we discussed the scales of the three types of 7th chords. We made the observation that chords and the scales played over them needed to be in agreement with each other, which gave us the term 'chord-scale relationship'. In the blues, this concept is not adhered to all that rigidly. The minor 7 blues scale can work over all three chords— *if* you choose to center your playing around note choices that control dissonance.

An example of this is the conflict between the 3 in the 7th chord and the b3 in the minor 7 blues scale. Playing the b3 in the scale over the natural 3 in the chord causes dissonance. While this dissonance has become a part of the sound of the blues, some players choose to resolve it using a few simple devices.

The minor 7 pentatonic scale can be brought into agreement with the 7th chord, but to do this the b3 needs to be replaced with a 3. While this will make the scale fit with the chord, the result just doesn't sound much like the blues. We're missing another one of those 'blue notes'. Instead of just replacing the b3 with the 3, the b3 is slurred *into* the 3. You can do this by either bending the b3 up ½ step or moving from b3 to 3 using a slide or hammer-on. Any of these techniques will move the b3 up ½ step to 3.

Diagram 153 shows an Amin7 pentatonic scale with b3 slurred to 3.
Diagram 154 shows the linear position of the Amin7 pentatonic scale with b3 slurred to 3.

Note: Remember, the reason for slurring the b3 into 3 is to bring the scale into agreement with the chord. This means that the upward slur from b3 to 3 is used even when playing the scale descending.

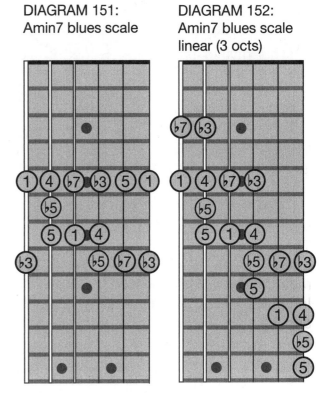

DIAGRAM 151:
Amin7 blues scale

DIAGRAM 152:
Amin7 blues scale
linear (3 octs)

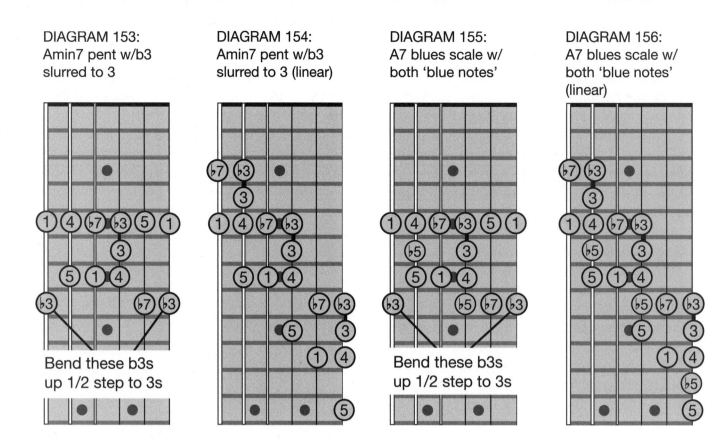

DIAGRAM 153:
Amin7 pent w/b3
slurred to 3

DIAGRAM 154:
Amin7 pent w/b3
slurred to 3 (linear)

DIAGRAM 155:
A7 blues scale w/
both 'blue notes'

DIAGRAM 156:
A7 blues scale w/
both 'blue notes'
(linear)

Bend these b3s
up 1/2 step to 3s

Bend these b3s
up 1/2 step to 3s

Adding the slur from b3 to 3 and adding the b5 as a passing note between 4 and 5 creates a _7th blues scale_. The 7th blues scale is shown in **Diagram 155**, and the linear position is in **Diagram 156**. The blue notes—b3 and b5—aren't seen as incorrect. Instead, they are the notes that give us the sound of the blues.

These scale shapes can be moved across the fingerboard to create the same scale types around root notes on the A string. Just remember to make the adjustment to compensate for the tuning of the B string.

PLAYING OVER THE BLUES CHORD PROGRESSION

So, how do we go about actually playing the blues? As previously mentioned, the minor 7 blues scale can be used to play over the chords in the blues progression. Experiment with this and see how it works. You may find that you are able to work around the dissonance between the b3 of the scale and the 3 of the chord by following your ear. This is a worthy and valid approach that many well-known players use.

There are, however, many different ways of approaching improvisation over the blues, each of which involves looking at chord-scale relationships. One of these involves playing within the blues scale of each chord as shown below:

Chords	**A7**	**D7**	**E7**
Scales	**A7 blues**	**D7 blues**	**E7 blues**

Think of this as _parallel playing_, or moving the same scale type to different root notes in order to play similar ideas over each chord. While this a completely valid approach, it takes a lot of thought to move from one scale to another.

There is another way to play over these changes that makes use of our knowledge of keys—modal playing. This type of playing involves using the scale(s) of chords from the key that are not the scale of the chord being played. This approach is more common than parallel playing and you will likely find it easier to use. (We will discuss modes in great detail in my next book, but for now let's get the basics down.)

As we discovered earlier, when the chord changes from A7 to D7, there has been a change of keys. The D7 chord is V of the key of G. Instead of changing to the D7 scale, let's see if we can stay in an A scale of some type.

Does the key of G have an A chord in it? Yes—A is the 2nd note in the G major scale. The chord built on the 2nd interval of any key is a minor 7 chord. Therefore, the II chord in the key of G is an Amin7 chord.

Rather than changing from the A7 blues scale to a D7 blues scale, it is much easier to acknowledge the key change by adjusting the A7 blues scale to fit the scale's relationship to the key of G.

In other words, you can play an Amin7 blues scale over the D7 chord! This means that the change from the A7 chord to the D7 chord can be acknowledged by centering around the b3 of the scale. Replacing the b3 with a 3 moves you back to the A7 chord, as shown below:

Chord	A7	D7	E7
Scale	A7 blues	Amin7 blues	Amin7 blues

The Amin7 blues scale is easier to use than parallel playing, and has the added advantage of allowing you to access language used more commonly by blues players.

But what about the E7 chord? Remember, the blues idiom evolved from a group of people who had little or no knowledge of theory concepts. Players chose what they played based solely on the way things sounded and felt. As we have discussed, the E7 chord is the V chord of the key of A. If we use the same logic that led us to playing the minor 7 blues scale over the D7 chord, the A major scale should work. You can try it, but you will notice that it just doesn't sound like the blues.

In the context of a 12-bar blues progression, the Amin7 blues scale is most commonly played over the V chord, E7. Playing in the scale of a chord not in the same key causes some dissonance. But, as the progression moves to the D7 chord, the dissonance is resolved by the move back to the key (G). Parallel playing is also an option: you can always play the E7 blues scale over the E7 chord.

Chord	A7	D7	E7
Scale	A7 blues	Amin7 blues	Amin7 blues

USING THE 'RELATIVE MINOR' SCALE IN THE BLUES

In the chapter on keys, we discussed the relative minor chord. The relative minor chord in any key is the VI chord. Looking at the VI chord's relationship to the I chord, we can see it occurs 1½ steps below the I chord. This is useful information, but made even more useful if we expand the relative minor concept to other places in a key.

Let's look at the IV chord. Is there a minor 7 chord 1½ steps below the IV chord? There is—the II chord. This means, if a IV chord is played, you can use the minor 7 pentatonic scale of the II chord to play over it.

Looking at the V chord (the only 7th chord in any key), you can see that it also has a 'relative minor' chord. That chord is found 1½ steps below the V chord—the III chord. You can play the minor 7 pentatonic scale based around the III chord as a substitution scale over the V.

This adds to the textures of sound that can be used in the blues.

Chord	A7	D7	E7
Scale	F#min7 blues	Bmin7 blues	C#min7 blues

These are the 'relative minor' scales that can be played with each chord in the blues progression. If you use parallel playing to navigate through these relative minor scales, you may find this is a little easier said than done. It is far more common to find an F# chord and scale that fit the change of keys when the D7 chord is played.

Here is the logic: The D7 chord is the V chord of the key of G. Is there an F# chord in the key of G? Yes—the VII chord, F#min7b5.

You can easily adjust the F#min7 pentatonic scale to fit this chord—just replace the 5 with a b5. We've already used the b5 as a passing note between 4 and 5. Now it has become a primary note and is used to the exclusion of the 5. You can think of this scale as a <u>min7b5 pentatonic scale</u>.

Diagram 157 shows the F#min7b5 pentatonic scale
Diagram 158 shows the same scale in open position on the E string and linear position on A string

Chords	A7	D7	E7
Scales	F#min7 blues	F#min7b5 blues	F#min7b5 pent.

The min7b5 pentatonic scale is also used over the E7 chord, even though it is not in the key of A. The change from the E7 to the D7 will resolve the dissonance.

So, the 'simple' blues is not so simple after all; there are many pathways available as you learn to improvise over the blues. Parallel playing, modal playing, the use of the relative minor scales and a combination of these approaches are all used by blues players.

The workbook will give you a list of these options and some suggestions on their use.

DIAGRAM 157:
F#min7b5
pentatonic scale

DIAGRAM 158:
F#min7b5
pentatonic scale
(linear)

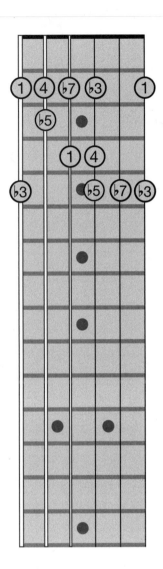

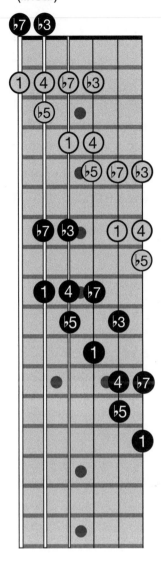

121

CHAPTER TEN - WORKBOOK

(NOTE: The Chapter Ten Workbook combines the Information, Visualization and Application sections)

PLAYING OVER BLUES CHANGES

Below you will find a list of chord-scale relationships for use when improvising over blues changes, followed by some examples of how to use them.

Example one

Chords	A7	D7	E7
Scales	Amin7 blues	Amin7 blues	Amin7 blues

Example two

Chords	A7	D7	E7
Scales	A7 blues	D7 blues	E7 blues

Example three

Chords	A7	D7	E7
Scales	A7 blues	Amin7 blues	Amin7 blues

Example four

Chords	A7	D7	E7
Scales	F#min7 blues	Bmin7 blues	C#min7 blues

Example five

Chords	A7	D7	E7
Scales	F#7min blues	F#min7b5 blues	F#min7b5 blues

Example one, using only the minor 7 blues scale, is the easiest. It will still take practice, however, to find the resolved notes. It is best to let your ear do most of the work. Record the blues progression and start by playing the Amin7 blues scale along with it ascending and descending, listening to the way the notes interact with the chords. Next, try moving around within the scale to find 'ideas' that work. Treat this as one part mental exercise and one part ear training; aimlessly wandering around in the scale is not going to give you the most satisfying results. Try to hear what you are going to play before (or as) you play it.

Example two uses parallel playing, or playing within the scale of each chord and changing scales as the chords change. This takes considerably more thought and movement than working with the minor 7 pentatonic scale alone. I would suggest saving this approach for later, after you have developed some facility with the examples that require fewer transitions from scale to scale.

Example three is much easier to use than the previous example and still acknowledges the change of chord and key. As we found in Chapter Ten, acknowledging the change between the I chord and the IV chord in a blues progression involves focusing on the 3 or b3 of the blues scale. First, get used to the A7 blues scale by playing it ascending and descending.

In a blues progression in A, the A7 chord is acknowledged by slurring the b3 into the 3 of the A7 blues scale. Using the b3 in the scale without slurring it into the 3 acknowledges the D7 chord (the b3 of the scale is the b7 of the D7 chord).

To get used to this, try recording two measures of the A7 blues rhythm followed by two measures of the D7 and repeating this several times. Then try playing over this simple progression. As the chords change, meet that change with the target note (the 3 or b3). As you improvise, work on playing ideas that meet those target notes. If you don't have a way to record yourself (a basic recording application in your computer or a 'looper' pedal will work just fine), find a friend who plays and trade off playing rhythm and soloing. Then try playing over the entire blues progression meeting the changes. You will have much more success with the entire progression if you pace yourself and don't skip this important intermediary step.

Example four shows parallel playing using the relative minor concept. As we saw in example two, parallel playing involves more thinking and more movement and is best saved for later.

Example five shows a simpler approach using the 'relative minor' chord that still acknowledges the chord/key change. Play the F#min7 blues scale over the A7 chord and play the min7b5 pentatonic scale over the D7 chord. The target points are different, emphasizing the 5 while the A7 is played and meeting the D7 chord with the b5.

These approaches can be mixed. For instance, you can play an F#min7 blues scale over the A7 chord and then change to the Amin7 blues scale over the D7 and E7 chords.

Another often-used combination is to play the A7 blues scale over the A7 chord and change to the F#min7b5 pentatonic scale over the D7 and E7 chords.

Remember—you can always improvise within the blues scale of the chord being played, but you are now able to make other choices as long as you engage your ears.

So much for the 'simple' blues. There are so many different options available to help you express yourself while playing. There are more, but we'll discuss those in the next book.

A BIT MORE ON IMPROVISATION

The art of improvising is an elusive thing. It involves much more than knowing which scales work in a particular musical situation—more than the physical mechanics involved in playing the scales. Improvising requires you to create melodies spontaneously—*to play your own ideas!* But where do these ideas come from?

There are two types of resources you can draw on when you improvise. I think of them as external resources and internal resources.

The external resources are the scale shapes and riffs that you have learned, or perhaps 'borrowed' from other players. You can find ideas by randomly moving around in a scale to see what happens. If you find something that works well, put that in your 'list of ideas' and call upon it as needed. This is a valid way to approach improvising. The randomness of this approach can lead you to surprising places as you search for ideas, some more musical than others.

The internal resources are a bit more elusive. They come from your ear—in a way. Using your internal resources means playing what you hear 'in your head'. This requires getting used to what it sounds like when you play a certain combination of notes and using these notes as a 'jumping off point' into other ideas. Put more simply, this might mean playing a certain note in the scale, and then training the fingers to find other notes that you hear in relation to that note.

<u>Sound a little confusing? Try this exercise:</u>

Play through a scale to warm up your hands and ears. Then, play the root note of the scale. Now, don't play another note until you can *sing it to yourself or hear it in your head.* Then find another note, and then another. Continue playing this way, always trying to hear what you are going to play before you play it. It will take some time to develop this ability, but the rewards of learning to play what you hear instead of hearing what you play are immeasurable.

<u>Here is another good way to develop your internal resources:</u>

Get together with another player, have them play a riff, and then try to find what they are playing, by following your ear. Then trade roles, and do the same for him or her. Start with short, simple phrases at first. The goal is to gradually close the gap between hearing an idea and being able to play it. This can help you learn to create melodies 'on the fly', and truly improvise spontaneously. This is a valuable tool for aspiring lead players and songwriters; ideas for songwriting often come as the result of improvisation.

Most players will use a combination of these resources. I love to improvise, to put some of myself into songs that I am playing. The times when I feel best about my improvising are those times when I move beyond thinking about the notes (external resources) and start playing what I hear (internal resources). Getting the brain out of the way is a good thing and can bear some surprising results.

Access to these internal resources is not always as immediate as we would like. Some days are better than others, so it is good to have a solid base of external resources (scales and riffs) that you can rely on at those times when spontaneous ideas don't come easily.

EPILOGUE

At this point in my life I can easily say I have committed my journey on this planet unequivocally to my relationship with the guitar. I have discovered that, for every thing I learn, I become aware of how much I have yet to learn. Every door that I open, if I choose to walk through that door, leads to a room with more doors. There is always more to discover, and each discovery leads us to even more unknowns.

'One man's journey toward understanding the guitar' is not meant to lead you to a final destination. I offer you no guarantees. But, I do hope to show you that the journey itself has *so much value*—that there can be a logical, methodical approach that can guide you as you move forward on this path.

We have come such a long way in ten simple chapters. It is my hope that, as you have studied the text in this book and worked with the exercises in the workbook sections, you have grown in your understanding of the guitar and have found a new way of viewing the fingerboard.

I am sure that many of you have, at this point, reached a level of saturation in your journey and need time to digest this information and make it your own before you move on— if you decide to move on. One of the amazing things about the guitar is its capacity to satisfy players of any skill level. The information covered in this book may be enough for you; it may even be more than you care to delve into for quite some time.

For those of you who are ready to fully explore the concepts we have covered, I am sure that many more questions will arise. Some of these questions may have been hinted at, but not answered completely at this point in the journey—questions like:

- What about modes? What are they? Where do they come from? How can they be used?

- If there are only 7 notes in a given scale, where do 9th, 11th and 13th chords come from?

- How do 7#5 chords or 7b5 chords—chords that appear to contain non-scale notes— fit into the picture?

- What does it mean if you see chords written as 'musical fractions': A/G, G/A, D7/F#, and so on?

- What are chord inversions and how are they fingered on the guitar? How and when can they be used?

- Are there true minor keys? What is meant by 'minor tonality'?

- How can I learn to improvise over complex chord progressions, like those in jazz songs?

- What about 'ethnic' or world music? What makes those different-sounding musical styles unique? What makes them similar to what we already know?

This book is but the beginning. It is meant to give you an understanding of the basic concepts of music theory, to give you a foundation to build upon so we can move forward toward answering these questions and many more.

The narrative of my personal journey, and my quest to find out *why* it all works, has stopped with me being in my early twenties. I have spent a lifetime walking down this pathway with my guitar, and there is much more of my journey to be shared.

This book is only the first step down a long and interesting path. Your ability to deal with the increasingly complex concepts we encounter along the way will be determined by how well you understand what we have dealt with in this first book. *Do not skip the basics!* It turns out the basics will become everything you need to know.

While you are beginning your own journey, it will help you greatly to learn to think in terms of intervals. If you can't look at any chord or scale that you know and see the intervals that make up that chord or scale, you don't really know it. You are simply repeating something you have learned, without gaining any true knowledge. Being able to hear and think in terms of intervals is the key to truly moving forward as a guitarist.

Thank you for letting me share my story and knowledge with you. I hope that we will continue our journey together in the next book.

In loving memory of Steve Maase, guitarist and educator, 1946-2016.

GLOSSARY

12-Bar Blues - A repeating chord progression that takes place over twelve measures using 7th chords in a I IV V sequence, most commonly:

```
|: I | IV | I | I |
| IV | IV | I | I |
| V | IV | I | V :|
```

7th Blues Scale - A modified version of the minor pentatonic scale that includes both the 'blue note' and a slur from flat 3 to 3, which brings the scale into agreement with 7th chords.

7th Chord - A chord with the b7 degree of a scale added to a major triad.

A form Chords and Scales - Chords and scales whose root notes are on the A string and follow the shape of an open A chord. The chords are played by barring across the fingerboard with the first finger.

Accidentals - Sharps (#) or flats (b) used to indicate notes found between the natural notes.

Arpeggio - A chord played one note at a time.

Bar Chord - A chord played by barring across the strings with the first finger so that the shape of an open chord can be played above it.

Blue Note - A note not found in the scale of a chord that is slurred into a chord note (b3 to 3) or used as a chromatic (½ step) passing note between two scale notes. Example; b5 is a passing note between 4 and 5.

Blues Scale - A version of the minor pentatonic scale modified to incorporate 'blue notes'.

C form Chords and Scales - Chords and scales whose root notes are found on the A string and follow the shape of an open C chord. The chords are played by barring across the fingerboard with the first finger.

Chord - Traditionally a group of three or more notes played together. In contemporary music, a chord (such as a power chord) is sometimes played with just two notes instead of three.

Chord-Scale Relationship - Referring to a scale and the chord(s) that can be found within it, or a chord and the scale that the chord comes from.

Chromatic Scale - A scale containing all twelve notes commonly found in the music of Western civilization.

Consonance - The sound of notes played together that are separated by distance in pitch (for example, two notes played a fifth apart).

Cross-Tuning - The process of tuning the guitar by finding a specific note on one string and using that note to tune the next highest open string.

D form Chords and Scales - Chords and scales whose root notes are found on the D string and follow the shape of an open D chord. The chords are often made by barring across the first four strings with the first finger.

Diatonic - Literally multi-tonal, having several notes. Generally used in reference to scales with seven notes.

Diatonic Scales - Scales comprised of seven different notes, especially the major scale and its derivatives.

Diminished Triad - A three-note chord comprised of the 1, b3 and b5 intervals of a scale.

Dissonance - The sound of notes that clash with each other, most often occurring when notes are played too close to each other in pitch (for example, two notes played ½ step apart).

E form Chords and Scales - Chords and scales whose root notes are found on the low E string and follow the shape of an open E chord. The chords are made by barring across the fingerboard with the first finger.

Economy of Movement - Finding chords or single notes that are close enough to each other in order to avoid excess movement from one hand position to the next.

Enharmonic - Notes (or chords) that can be called by two different names. For example, A# and Bb are enharmonic notes; both occupy the ½ step interval between A and B.

F form Chords and Scales - Chords and scales whose root notes are found on the D string and follow the shape of an open F chord.

G form Chords and Scales - Chords and scales whose root notes are found on the low E string and follow the shape of an open G chord. The chords are made by barring across the fingerboard with the first finger.

Hand Position - A 'four-fret span' played using four fingers, with each fret being played by one of the four fingers. Also refers to the 'proper' positioning of the left hand with the thumb behind the neck, straight, parallel to the frets, allowing easy access to the four-finger, four-fret position. This position also facilitates barring across the fingerboard when making bar chords.

Intervals - The numbered degrees of a scale or chord.

Keys - The major scales which can be started from any of the twelve notes of the chromatic scale. The keys are named by the first note in the scale.

The Major Scale - Any of a number of scales containing seven different notes that follow a formula of whole steps and half steps as follows: whole, whole, half, whole, whole, whole, half.

Major Seventh Chord - A chord built upon a major triad with the seventh degree of the scale added to it, described as the intervals 1, 3, 5, and 7.

Major Triad - A three-note chord made up of the 1, 3, and 5 degrees of a major scale.

Min7b5 Chord - A chord made of the 1, b3, b5, and b7 degrees of a scale.

Min7b5 Pentatonic Scale - A minor 7 pentatonic with the 5 replaced by a b5.

Minor 7 Chord - A chord made of the 1, b3, 5, and b7 degrees of a scale.

Minor Triad - A three-note chord made of the 1, b3, and 5 degrees of a scale.

Modal Playing - A type of playing that involves using the scale(s) of chords from the key that are not the scale of the chord being played.

Open Position - Chords and scales played in first three frets of the guitar, often using open strings.

Parallel Playing - In a given chord progression, moving a melodic idea played in the scale of one chord to the scale of the next chord.

Pentatonic Scale - Scales using 5 different notes, most commonly used in reference to the minor 7 pentatonic scale: 1, b3, 4, 5, and b7.

Power Chord - A chord with only 1s and 5s.

Relative Minor - A minor or minor 7 chord that has notes in common with the I chord of a key. The VI chord of a key is the relative minor chord of the I chord of any key. Amin7 is the relative minor chord of the key of C. The Amin7 chord contains a C major triad. It is worth noting that every major chord in a key will have a relative minor scale.

Resolution - In a chord or scale, the movement of dissonant notes to consonance.

Root Note - The note that a chord or scale is built upon. In other words, the note that indicates the letter name of a chord or scale.

Shuffle Feel - An eighth-note triplet rhythm in which the first and third beats are played, while the second beat is omitted.

Substitution Scale - A scale other than the scale of a chord that is used to improvise over that chord. For example, the relative minor 7 pentatonic scale can be used to play over a major chord 1½ steps above.

Suspended Chord - A chord in which the 3 of a chord is replaced by a neighboring note (2 or 4).

Sus2 Chord - A chord in which the 3 of a chord is replaced by a 2.

Sus4 chord - A chord in which the 3 of a chord is replaced by a 4.

Thirds - Every other note in a scale. For example: 1 and 3, 2 and 4, 3 and 5 are notes are all one third apart. A major third is made up of two whole steps, and a minor third is made up of 1½.

Transposing - Moving the notes or chords in a song to another key while maintaining the relationship of the notes to each other in the new key.

Triplet - Rhythmically, a group of three notes or beats that occupy the space normally filled by two.

Turnaround - This is a literal way of describing the measure (or measures) at the end of a repeated chord progression in order to 'turn it around' to the beginning.

Voice Leading - The way that notes in one chord move into the notes in the following chord.

Voicing - The order in which the notes in a chord are positioned. For example, an A form E chord is voiced 1 5 1 3 5, while a C form E chord is voiced 1 3 5 1 3. They are both E chords but are voiced differently.

ACKNOWLEDGMENTS

There are three people to thank, above all else, for stepping in to save this project at a point where I might otherwise have been too overwhelmed to see it through: Scott Friedlander, who oversaw the layout of this book from start to finish; Wes Jones, who diligently saw to it that each diagram my father had drawn would be clean, clear, and ready for print; and Alan Boyes, whose skill as a technical reader brought the final details together before publication.

But, before this book got to these final stages, an amazing number of people appeared in my family's life to look after my father and myself. Each of them is worthy of the deepest gratitude for supporting me so that I, in turn, could do what it took to support my father and finish his life's work:

To Marcelo Gallegos for the hand-drawn cover art, which was framed and given to my father as a 70th birthday gift just before he passed; to Marita Weil for not just the beautiful portraits of my father, but for stepping in as liaison between my family and the medical examiner and police department while I was en route to New Mexico from New York, and for driving cross-country with me in a box truck packed with my father's instruments; to my sister Arielle, her partner Brandon, and our aunts and uncles for traveling to Albuquerque at a moment's notice to help attend to my father's final affairs; and to my dear friends Nima Jamshidi, Dustin Kiska and Amanda Boutz, whose food, hospitality and comfort in the first few weeks made such a sudden and unexpected loss possible to survive.

Special thanks go out to my childhood friend Jon Sakura, who looked after PJ, my father's cat, for seven months while I worked on the final layout of this book; to Rose Day for additional assistance with proofreading; to Tim Pierce for continuing to lend his support to this project from afar; to Jim Mooney, Pat Houlihan, and Gerry Greenhouse for looking after my father's archival materials and tools; and lastly to Joe Bonamassa and Norman's Rare Guitars for taking in a selection of my father's equipment for lutherie and repairs.

Beyond that, I would like to thank the hundreds of students that have passed through my father's studio, and the many more that have passed through mine, for showing my pops and I how to teach. Each and every one of you has been a blessing in my life, and I have learned so much from all of you. Thank you.

And of course, the deepest gratitude to my father, the inimitable Steve Maase, for showing me how to be the person and guitarist I am today. Thanks, Dad, for everything. I love you.